Dear Parent

What Every Child Wished Their Parents Knew

KEITH A. CRAFT

with Josh Craft, Keela Craft Ambrose & Whitney Craft Jones

Copyright © 2023 Keith A. Craft.

All rights reserved. No part of this publication may be reproduced, distrib-uted, or transmitted in any form or by any means, including photocopying, recording, or other electronic or mechanical methods, without the prior written permission of the publisher, except in the case of brief quotations embodied in critical reviews and certain other noncommercial uses permitted by copyright law. For permission requests, write to the publisher, addressed "Attention: Per-missions Coordinator," at the address below.

Unless noted otherwise, scriptures are taken from the NEW KING JAMES VERSION (NKJV): Scripture taken from the NEW KING JAMES VER-SION®. Copyright© 1982 by Thomas Nelson, Inc. Used by permission. All rights reserved.

Scriptures marked NLT are taken from the HOLY BIBLE, NEW LIVING TRANSLATION (NLT): Scriptures taken from the HOLY BIBLE, NEW LIVING TRANSLATION, Copyright© 1996, 2004, 2007 by Tyndale House Foundation. Used by permission of Tyndale House Publishers, Inc., Carol Stream, Illinois 60188. All rights reserved. Used by permission. Scriptures marked NIV are taken from the NEW INTERNATIONAL VERSION (NIV): Scripture taken from THE HOLY BIBLE, NEW INTERNATIONAL VER-SION ®. Copyright© 1973, 1978, 1984, 2011 by Biblica, Inc.™. Used by per-mission of Zondervan Scriptures marked KJV are taken from the KING JAMES VERSION (KJV): KING JAMES VERSION, public domain. Scriptures marked ESV are taken from the THE HOLY BIBLE, ENGLISH STANDARD VERSION (ESV): Scriptures taken from THE HOLY BIBLE, ENGLISH STANDARD VERSION ® Copyright© 2001 by Crossway, a publishing minis-try of Good News Publishers. Used by permission.

Printed in the United States of America.

Second Edition

First printing edition 2024.

ISBN: 979-8-3492-3179-7

Empire Publishing
www.empirebookpublishing.com

DEDICATION

To my PRECIOUS wife, Sheila. You are absolutely the greatest gift God could have given me. It is my deepest pleasure and privilege to be able to experience this life together with you. You are the greatest wife, mother, and "Peppis" in the whole world and I am honored God chose me to be your husband.

Thank you for your inspiration, your understanding, your perseverance, and most of all, your unconditional love. You're the best part of me!

CONTENTS

Dedication — III

About the Author — VI

Why I Wrote This Book — VII

The Purpose of This Book — X

A Special Word to Fathers — XI

A Special Word to Mothers — XVII

A Special Word to Single Parents — XXII

Introduction
A Note from Your Child — 1

I need you to love me
because this world is an unlovely place. — 5

Please be a good example
I need someone to follow. — 29

Please don't penalize me for being a child
I need room to grow! — 67

Spend time with me
we don't have much time together. — 101

I need you to be a person of commitment
because I need to learn the value of tenacity. — 135

I need you to be disciplined
because I need to be discipled. — 173

I need you to know who you are
so you can show me who I am. — 205

Conclusion
A Final Word to Parents — 213

ABOUT THE AUTHOR

As a thought leader, speaker, author, and pastor, Keith A. Craft shares his practical approach to leadership with thousands of leaders around the world.

He challenges and inspires others with his real-life stories, energetic humor and enduring principles that he backs up with his authentic, inside-out approach to leadership. His expertise is broad, spanning the topics of leadership, attitude, personal growth, teamwork, relationships and success, all through a biblical worldview.

WHY I WROTE THIS BOOK

September 2023

I wrote this book 32 years ago while my children were still children. Now, all three of them are adults, parents, and leaders in their own right. Sheila and I are celebrating 40 years of marriage, and over 583 months of dating as of writing this.

My first two, Joshua and Keela, graduated from ORU with degrees in Communications. Joshua Co-Pastors with me and his mom at Elevate Life Church where I am the Lead Pastor.

Keela is also a Pastor on staff and is our Leadership Development Pastor. She also helps host my Think Coach online group coaching and in-person Masterminds.

Whitney, our youngest, graduated high school at 16 with the intention of "bringing worship to the world." She and her husband, Clay, are doing just that together at our church. They lead not only our worship department, but our entire creative team.

Joshua and his wife Courtnei have three daughters: Charlie (5), Harper (3), and Daisy born in September 2023.

Keela and her husband Cole have two sons, Arik (3) and Kaln (1).

Clay and Whitney have two daughters, Layla (8) and Livy (6), and a son Clayton Taylor born October

2023. Throughout this book, they will share their perspective on how my parenting philosophy has shaped them, and is shaping their children.

I wrote this book when I was 31. Joshua was 5, Keela was 4, and Whitney was 2. This book was originally written for a potential book deal with a large publisher and I decided not to release it.

32 years ago - similar to today - there were a lot of unmarried people who gave marriage advice, poor people giving financial advice, and people who weren't parents giving parenting advice. Instead of joining this same group of theoretical "experts," I wanted to see if my parenting philosophy actually worked in my own family first.

With that said, Dear Parent was written but remained unpublished for my children's entire upbringing. I have left everything in this book the same as it was when I wrote it at the age of 31. The only additions and edits I have made to this book have been this passage, updating the statistics on fatherhood in the Introduction, a word to Single Parents, Chapter 7, and the Conclusion.

My children are the fruit of this parenting philosophy. Again, this is why I waited 32 years to publish this book. I have waited not only for them to "grow up", but become parents themselves. I had a dream at 31, that someday my children would comment honestly and openly on this philosophy, and they have done that. I believe that fruit always speaks louder than the seed. Fruit doesn't lie. Ultimately, it is not the theory or even philosophy that speaks, but it is THE FRUIT...that is THE PROOF!

My wife, Sheila, and I have made our best and imperfect efforts to raise our children in a way that pleases God. It has not been easy, but it has been worth it. We are in the greatest season of our life, seeing our children serve God, have children of their own, and choose to do life with us. I am confident that the same can, and will happen for you with your children.

The **Greatest Assignment** on this side of eternity that you will ever have is to reproduce the "Godness" in you, in your children! I pray this book will resource you. I pray this book will encourage you. I pray this book will help you elevate your thinking, so you can elevate your life and be empowered to elevate the lives of your children. I pray this book will serve as both a testimony and a template for you.

Believing God's BEST for you and your dear family,

Keith

THE PURPOSE OF THIS BOOK

The purpose of this book is 3-fold:
1. All of my life, I grew up hearing that no one is ever taught how to be a parent. Age, season of life, and even a desire for children, are not qualifiers for raising children. What then qualifies someone to be a parent? A desire to love and nurture a child, accompanied with a desire to Be the Best you can be in life. So, this book is written to inspire you to love and nurture your child, and to inspire you to Be the Best you can be as a person.

2. This book is written to hopefully help open the parent's eyes to a child's understanding and their view of the world. As parents, it is easy to forget the special gift that children are from the Lord, not to add pain and sorrow, but joy and fulfillment to the life of a person.

3. Children are the Future. The world will be a better place to live in, if we do a better job of raising our children.

Children are the greatest gift that God gives to you as a parent and to the world as a gift from God! And you, as a parent, are their greatest resource. You are the example that they will follow. I trust this book will help you. I hope it will inspire you to be better. I believe that it will give you insight into parenting and more importantly, a child's view and what their unspoken desires really are in a parent.

Keith A. Craft - 1991

A SPECIAL WORD TO FATHERS

I once heard someone say, *"Being a good man is hard. Being a good husband is difficult. But being a good father is the most difficult task of all."* What is a Father? Webster says, *"one who has begotten a child."* While this definition is true, a good father is so much more than this.

Abraham Lincoln is famously quoted as saying, *"All that I am, or hope to be, I owe to my angel mother."*

That is a wonderful sentiment, but many people don't know the relationship that Lincoln had with his father. His father Thomas, routinely physically abused him for the slightest mistake, and actively tried to prevent him from attending school or reading books. His father was not present at his wedding, and never met Abraham's wife or children. And Abraham did not attend his father's funeral and would not pay for a headstone for his grave.

Here's some recent stats on fathering in America:

- Almost 1/3 of children in the US live without a father in their home. (US Census Bureau)
- 63% of youth suicides are from fatherless homes (US Dept. Of Health/Census)
- 90% of all homeless and runaway children are from fatherless homes (US Dept. Of Health/Census)
- 85% of all children who show behavior

disorders come from fatherless homes (Center for Disease Control)

- 71% of all high school dropouts come from fatherless homes (National Principals Association Report)
- 71% of pregnant teenagers lack a father. (U.S. Department of Health and Human Services)
- 85% of youths in prisons grew up in a fatherless home. (Fulton County Georgia jail populations, Texas Department of Corrections)
- Fatherless boys and girls are: twice as likely to drop out of high school; twice as likely to end up in jail; four times more likely to need help for emotional or behavioral problems. (US D.H.H.S. news release)

These are just the stats on whether a father is physically present or not. Not whether they are a good father, or a good man. That's even rarer than having a father in the home.

Ask yourself this question, **"What is a good father?"** A good father is someone who assumes a role greater than himself, by taking responsibility for being the best he can be, for the benefit of another, his child.

In PROVERBS 29, the Bible tells us that "WITHOUT VISION, PEOPLE PERISH." What these statistics show is that a father is the chief visionary for his family and his children. Your chief responsibility is to have a great vision for your life. If you have a great vision for your life, you will have a great vision for your family; if you have a great vision for your family, you will have a great vision for your children. The vision you have, or don't have for your children, will ultimately determine one of the most important things about them, their identity.

A good father is a man who takes responsibility to help his children discover, develop, and deploy their God-given identity and purpose.

The role of your children's mother is to create a nurturing environment where your children can be developed.

Your role is to develop them. Without development, nurturing turns into over-nurturing, which creates insecure and dependent adults. Without nurturing, development becomes over-coaching where your children will base their value in life solely on performance.

There are many reasons being a good father is so difficult. Most men do not grow up with good role models for fathers, and therefore, the definition of manhood and the role of the father, is never quite understood.

Another problem is that most men evaluate their own manhood based on what they do in life. They see life through the myopic view of their achievements, occupation, and position, rather than focusing on who they really are and who they want to become. Their self-worth is based on their position in life, rather than who they are as a person. They don't see themselves as God sees them, they see themselves as other people see them.

Many men also misunderstand their role in their children's life, because they don't understand the role God actually gave them. They see themselves as being authoritative and they tend to operate from a position of power, rather than being the loving and caring father that their children need.

For many men, intimacy, the ability to be known deeply and personally, is difficult. Men are expected in our society to keep their feelings to themselves. Any show of emotion, outside of the sports arena, is deemed as weakness. Culture has often taught us that vulnerability is the highest form of this weakness.

Again, there are many reasons being a good father is so difficult. I want to encourage you to understand that you can be any kind of father you want to be. This book is to, hopefully, help you know what your children need from you. Remember, you cannot love your children too much. You cannot show your children too much affection. You will not harm them by being the best father that you can possibly be.

If you had a bad father, use the lack you experienced with your own father to help you know what not to do. If you had a good father, use the good in your father to help you know what to do better. No matter what you do, remember this: The greatest influence on a child's self-image is a close relationship with their father.

Always remember, the greatest thing you can do for your children as their father, is to BE A MAN OF GOD. Make decisions and live your life based on the principles found in God's word, the Bible. Your commitment to do this will protect your spirit and soul and will also protect your children.

The second greatest thing you can do for your children is to love their mother, your wife. Your children did not choose you, you chose to have them. This is a tremendous responsibility. Every choice that you make in life from the point these children are conceived will directly affect them. You need to take this seriously and solemnly. Remember this, no matter what you do, one day your children's lives will remind you how your choices affected them.

Your child's self-worth will be in direct relationship to how you see yourself. If you realize your own value, then you will make decisions that will increase your value as a person, and the value that your children place on their own lives will be in direct proportion to the value you place on yourself.

The consequences of making bad choices when you have children, goes way beyond what happens to you. Your bad choices will hurt your children forever. The good news is that your good choices will bless your children forever! You get to decide the choices you make. And in deciding the choices you make, you are deciding what your children will experience in their future. The role you play is of utmost importance.

One word about divorce and children outside of marriage. If you have had children by someone who you are not currently married to, don't ever make your children your negative sounding board. Making someone else look bad to your child, will actually only make you look bad. And in many cases, the child feels uncomfortably caught in the middle, hearing bad about both from both sides, and yet loving both. Your negativity will breed in your children insecurity, doubt, and lack of respect for marriage and authority. This permanently scars children for life.

If you have already engaged in this negative type behavior, I want to encourage you to apologize to your child and let them know it will never happen again. The only exception to this would be, if a child would be in danger from being around this person.

Even if you are divorced, or unmarried to the other parent of your children, you are still their parent. You will never stop being their parent. Your situation may be difficult, but you can still be the best person/parent you can be starting right now.

A SPECIAL WORD TO MOTHERS

It is amazing to me the difference in the definition Webster gives for father and mother.

A mother is not someone who has simply "begotten a child" but a mother "gives birth or life to a child." A mother, Webster says, is "the maternal source of tenderness and affection."

I find the comparison of how Webster defines a father's role and a mother's role very interesting. I also find it typical and unfortunate that most men see their role as less significant than a woman's in raising children. All one needs to do to find that this is a modern day myth, is to interview a few prisoners behind bars. God never intended for children to be raised by a single parent, father or mother. This statement is not meant to condemn you if you are a single parent, but you must be alerted to the fact that all children need the influence of male and female parents.

Unfortunately, in the world we live today, the vast majority of single parents are mothers. Very few women are raising children alone because the husband has died. Most single women are raising children alone, because the father has abdicated his role as a father.

As a mother, you are vitally important. You wouldn't be reading this book if you weren't already a parent or were soon to be one, so there are a few things I would like to say to you:

First, you set the tone in your home. You carried these children for 9 months, your home is an incubator, just like a womb. The environment you create will be healthy or unhealthy. Therefore, your children will grow healthy or unhealthy because of you. Your emotional state will be the state of your family. The decision you make to be healthy mentally, emotionally, and spiritually will create a loving and peaceful home. If you are unhealthy, you will create an unhealthy environment that will stunt the growth of your children.

Secondly, the greatest and most difficult job you will ever have is in the home. It is my opinion - and I do mean opinion - that after speaking to millions of young people, the best-rounded and most confident young people come from homes where mothers are home.

Don't misunderstand me. I am not asserting that the only place a woman has is in the home. But you, as a woman, are the nurturer and builder of the home your children live in. That is not your husband's primary responsibility, nor does a man necessarily possess that ability. God created men and women radically different. And He was intentional in His creation. If you choose to have children, the best place you can be is in the home. Of course, you can be anywhere you want to be, and do anything you want to do. You don't need my permission or approval. But, by having children, you have decided - maybe without realizing it - that being a mother is the greatest role you can play on this earth. If a woman finds more fulfillment in doing her job outside of the home than she does being a mother, she is deceived and has lowered herself to a wrong mentality that most men have: finding their self-esteem based on what they are doing, rather than who they already are and are becoming. Furthermore, it is my opinion that this type of woman never should have become a mother in the first place. The feminist who says "I am WOMAN, hear me roar!" will vehemently disagree with me. She will say, "You have no right to speak for or to any woman, because you are a man, and besides, why can't a woman have the best of both worlds?"

There is no such thing as the best of both worlds. You're trying to create a world where you get what you want, and your children get what they need. You can't always do both at once. One will suffer for the other. The best world you can live in is the world you create for your children, by being there for them–not the world you seek to create for yourself.

My opinion is based upon the fact that I have spoken to millions of kids in hundreds of junior high schools and high schools all across America; and my own personal experience growing up. My mother and father both worked so that we could have more things. The reality was, we got less of them and whatever the "more" was because my mother worked. We lived in a very modest house that cost $19,000 with a $76 dollar monthly payment. We ate at home most of the time. In fact, I only remember going out for dinner on Sundays after church. We did not wear name brand anything. We lived in the same house in a lower middle class neighborhood and my parents never had a new car. We did take a few local vacations within driving distance. I don't ever remember staying in a hotel. My mamaw lived with us so they had in-house childcare. I am still to this day not sure why my mom worked outside the home.

I do not say any of the aforementioned to speak negatively about my parents, but what I wanted most as a child was more of them. A little bigger house, a newer car, and all the other things that parents work so hard for, do not matter to children half as much as being with their parents. If you work, work. But make sure that your children are your first priority with your time, otherwise, you will not create the right kind of home environment to raise your children in.

The greatest influences I have had in my life have been women. My mother taught me to pray. My Mamaw - my mother's mother - is my hero. She showed me what it was like to live for God. I am absolutely grateful for the gift of them in my life. But, that is not God's design. Women can, and should be our heroes. But as a man, I needed the voice of a father in my life. Men have not taken their proper place in the home and in the church, and this makes your job that much harder. I wish I could apologize to you for this, but I can't speak for other men. I can speak for myself, and as a man, tell you to be encouraged because you are and can continue to make a difference in this world. If you are a single female parent reading this book, I encourage you to stand strong. I've watched hundreds of football games and I have never seen one player thank his dad. It's always, "Hi Mom, I Love You, Thanks."

Expose your children to male role models, preferably Christian men, and at this point, put their needs before your own, when choosing a man. Find a tribe of Godly men you can surround your children with who will encourage them, love them, and mentor them. Most likely, what will be the best for them, will also be the best for you.

A SPECIAL WORD TO SINGLE PARENTS

Your role as a single parent is critically important and extremely challenging. You are the provider, the nurturer, the role model, and the CEO of your family. You often play the role of father and mother and I want to encourage you in your journey.

The best thing you can do is find a strong support system around you to help you. No matter what the issues are that have put you in a position to be a single parent, you must remember that your kids are God's children and He has a great plan for them.

I have always taught that family of choice is more powerful than family of origin — and that extends to your children. You can help them choose spiritual mothers and spiritual fathers who will speak into them and help to fill any gap that you see in their family of origin. That is why you need to be in a "household of faith." God calls the church a family, and the family of God that you choose for your children is vitally important when you are a single parent. You may be alone right now in parenting your child, but you won't be alone when you get deeply connected in God's family on earth, the church. Don't allow yourself to feel guilty and isolated. Pursue finding your family of choice and you will see God's plan for your kids come to pass.

Develop a vision for your family and write core values.

As a single parent, your hands can get full quickly and easily. Our family mission statement is "never allow the good to be robber of the best." And our family core values are: honor, positive attitude, excellence, and generosity. Your vision and core values will guide you and set the tone for your family, even when you feel overwhelmed by the challenges that only you may face.

Fight to create balance between authority and nurture, between law and love. It is a tough balancing act to go between being the "mom" and "dad." Your children actually will have a unique opportunity from an early age. They can learn to serve your family better than other kids and take care of their own age-appropriate needs. Don't do everything for your kids; teach them to do chores, clean their rooms, and become self-reliant. That's what any good parent does, single or otherwise. Your kids may have to be self-reliant a lot younger than other kids, but that will most often be an advantage they will have over kids their age, if you let it. Don't do everything for your kids, but help them process these things emotionally. Love them through the process of development that is taking place. Correct your kids, but don't do it out of frustration; correct them out of love and express to them the purpose of the correction. The purpose of all corrections with children is that you want the best for them and you are the one person who will always have their best interests in mind. Do your best to express this to them every time they require your correction.

Develop your — and their — self-esteem. Your worth is not tied to being in a two-parent household, and neither is theirs. Nothing in your life is more important than how you see yourself. Nothing in your children's life is more important than how you see them. Demonstrate a lot of love to them verbally and nonverbally. Use frequent and sincere praise. Show your children unconditional love, but don't expect it from them. They need your help to learn how to love you and love themselves. Here's three things you and your children need to develop self esteem:

1. **A tribe**
   Everyone needs to belong to something bigger than themselves. You can help your children develop self-esteem by making yourself - and them - a part of something bigger than your family. This is why churches exist.

2. **Self discipline**
   You must develop the discipline to control what you can control. Your thinking, being (attitude), and doing will always determine what you have in life. When you learn to be self-disciplined, you open the door to self-discovery, which breeds self-confidence, which develops self-competence that will help you reach self-mastery. Focus on what you can control in your life and believe that will be enough. It is all you can do anyway. When you show your

children what this looks like, it's like a superpower within your family.

3. **Your (and their) 1%**
   Self-discipline leads to self-discovery. Only through discipline can you begin to discover the greatness that already is within you. I wrote a book called *Your Divine Fingerprint* on how to discover this, but you need to understand who you are and help your kids do the same. You have a fingerprint that no one else has to leave an imprint no one else can leave. If you understand this, you will be glad that you're you. Because you're the only person on the planet who can leave the imprint God gave you to leave. If you don't think you're great, your kids won't either. Discover, develop, and deploy your greatness so that you can teach your kids to do the same.

THIS IS VERY IMPORTANT: Always choose to honor the other parent, even if you don't have much of a relationship. Make sure your children understand that the absence of the other parent is not their fault. Also choose to never speak negatively about the other parent in front of your kids. Your children will often take this criticism and apply it to themselves. After all, they are their children too. Don't allow your negative interactions with the other parent to taint the perspective of your children. Speak to your children about the other parent in an age-appropriate way and allow your kids to love the other parent if at all possible. If negative interactions take place between your child and the other parent, help your children work through it without being negative and critical of the other parent. If you have a co-parent, strive to create consistent vision and values across both households and do whatever you can to have a healthy working relationship.

Finally, and most importantly, be the best you that only you can be. You will be a great parent if you are a great person. Develop yourself personally and it will affect your parenting in a positive way. Your emotional, spiritual, physical, and spiritual health is crucial to your family's well being. Don't neglect yourself or try to do the impossible. Do the best you can in every season you are in, and lean on your family of choice.

Proverbs 3:5-6 says: "TRUST IN THE LORD WITH ALL YOUR HEART, AND LEAN NOT ON YOUR OWN UNDERSTANDING; IN ALL YOUR WAYS ACKNOWLEDGE HIM, AND HE SHALL DIRECT YOUR PATHS." When all else fails, trust God, and He will direct your family's path to the great plan He has for you and your children.

Introduction

A Note from Your Child

Dear Parent:

I want to begin by saying how much I love you. You did not have to teach me to love you. I love you because of who you are to me, my Parent. This is not hard for me because from the very beginning I have loved you. My ultimate goal in life is to be loved and accepted by you.

There are many reasons for this book. But the primary reason is because I want you to know how I feel and what is important to me at this point in my life.

You are the greatest influence in my life. Everything you do affects me. I am watching you very closely; how you act and how you react. Webster says that a parent is "a source from which other things are derived." It is from you that I learn what is acceptable and what is unacceptable. Your values are becoming my values. How you see the world directly affects my world view.

What you envision for me, I will eventually envision for myself. At this point in my life, I am seeing the world through your eyes. If you choose to be positive, I will be positive. If you choose to be negative, I will be negative. I will imitate your behavior. I will impersonate your character. I will assimilate your worldview of me.

I also want you to understand that we don't have much time together. I will not be a child forever. We may have 18 short years together, but then really only God knows if we have that long. I want us to make the best of this time. It is so important to me. For you see, we really only have today. We have no assurance of a tomorrow.

Please try to remember, I am only a child. I did not ask to come into this world, however, I am glad I did or I would have never met you. I really think you're the greatest. Only you can ever convince me otherwise.

As you read this book, I hope it affects you as much as you affect me. It is hard for me to communicate all of my feelings to you. Words don't come easy for me just now, but I am learning because I am watching you. What you say about me and to me is how I will feel about you. When you feel good about me, I feel good about you. And when I feel good about you, I will feel good about myself!

One more thing about influence. Your influence in my life will leave its mark forever. It is something you will never be able to change, nor will I. Once you have exerted the power you have to influence me, it will be permanent. Good or bad. Think about it: I may even have children someday, and the influence you had on me will directly affect the influence I have on them. God has placed you in the most honorable position you can ever have on this earth and that is to be a Parent: to be a source from which other lives will be derived.

> YOUR INFLUENCE IN MY LIFE WILL LEAVE ITS MARK FOREVER. IT IS SOMETHING YOU WILL NEVER BE ABLE TO CHANGE, NOR WILL I.

Always remember, I love you. I am watching you because I want to be just like you. There is one thing you can count on: I will be the one person in this world that truly demonstrates your character and the true influence you really have on this world. I am your offspring. I am the seed you have sown on this earth. I am the fruit of your life.

Your Child.

1

I need you to love me

because this world is an unlovely place.

Dear Parent:

The most important thing I will ever need from you is your unconditional LOVE. It is important that I know that I can never do anything that would cause you to stop loving me. There will be few people in my life who will ever truly love me simply because of who I am. The world will measure my significance based upon my performance. I need you to love me regardless.

There are FOUR things about love that speak to me the most: ACCEPTANCE, APPRECIATION, AFFECTION, and APPROVAL.

ACCEPTANCE

I need your love for me expressed through your acceptance of me for who I am – your child. Your ability to accept me for who I am will be reflected in my ability to accept myself. I cannot be someone whom I am not, but I can be me. I need you to help me be the best me that I can be. The most important way in which you can do that is to help me to discover myself, by focusing on my strengths and helping me to overcome my weaknesses. I don't need you to continually point out the areas where you feel that I am weak. I need you to accept me for me and love me enough that you commit yourself to my personal development.

> YOUR ABILITY TO ACCEPT ME FOR WHO I AM WILL BE REFLECTED IN MY ABILITY TO ACCEPT MYSELF.

To ACCEPT means to UNDERSTAND. I need you to try to understand me. Understand that I am only a child. I will act like a child; I will talk like a child; I will play like a child; I will eat like a child; I will fuss from time to time like a child; I will be messy like a child. In other words, I will spill my milk every once in a while. When this happens, I need you to communicate to me that accidents happen and everybody spills their milk every once in a while. So please don't teach me to cry over spilled milk. Accept me, please.

Your Child

JOSH

One of the greatest things my parents did for me was to accept me as I was. I could not be more opposite from my dad. Most of the time in families when fathers and sons are different, there is more conflict than growth, there are more feelings of rejection than understanding and acceptance.

One of the greatest things my Dad ever did, and still tries to do, is to understand me. He's always led me, and steered me, but I cannot remember a time that he has done that because it was about what he wanted me to do. He didn't seek to shape me into his image, but to help me become the best me that he knew I had the potential to be. He wanted me to realize I was God's son first, and his son second. I was not created in the image of Keith Craft. I was created in the image of God. And God put me in this particular family so He could shape me into who He created me to be.

I have always been accepted, but at the same time, I always knew that there was a better way. I am meant for more than my personality, or default ways of thinking.

Growing up - like many kids - I had a new interest just about every 6 months or so, and these interests would wane quickly. As I am realizing with my own children, most of these interests and activities come with significant financial investment. In the midst of these ever-changing interests, my parents saw that their role was to invest in my interests.

I don't remember being told, "We can't afford that," or "No, son, you can't do that." The response I saw from my parents was usually something like: "Whatever you decide to do, we will support you as much as we possibly can." Being older, I see how much of an investment that was for them to make in me, and how much they

I need you to love me

valued my own journey of discovering things that I enjoyed, and could be passionate about.

There was one particular time when I decided to try my hand at Taekwondo. I was around eight or nine at the time, and my dad took me. The first class I attended was just right for me as an introvert - small and intimate. I had a great time at my first lesson. A week later we went back for the second lesson and it seemed like they had tripled the class size. There was also a different teacher and I didn't recognize anyone! In my mind, this was not okay. "How can I learn in an environment where there's so many people watching me, and so many people I don't know." About half way through the class, I decided I didn't want to do Taekwondo anymore and told my dad. - The reason I remember this story so well is this exact moment - My dad said, "Son, it's alright if you decide that you don't like Taekwondo, but if you decide to leave now, we aren't coming back, and you'll never know what you missed out on."

That lesson has stuck with me for more than twenty years (I'm 36 as of writing this). My dad embraced me and accepted me, and at the same time taught me one of his leadershipologies that says, "Whatever you resist, you cannot benefit from." I felt fully accepted by my dad in that situation, yet at the same time, since that day I've been acutely aware of the price I have to pay when I decide to quit something.

KEELA

While I didn't feel understood at every moment in my family, I always felt accepted. I am the middle child, and because of my wiring, I sometimes felt like an outsider in my family. I went through specific things growing up that my siblings did not, and because of this, I had a unique journey – (as we all do) in building self-confidence and trust in God. I think that disappointing someone is a natural fear that we all carry. I never wanted to let my parents down or be someone who was constantly messing up. I am not a people pleaser, but I want to win. Growing up, my mom and dad were honest about where I needed to grow and improve, but just as often, they spoke about what I did well and what I was good at. This helped me have a balanced view of myself and let me know where I could work to improve.

When I was in high school, there was a situation that happened that I thought was going to upset my dad so much. Our house had a steep driveway with large, sharp rocks lining the edges. I was coming home one day and accidentally got too close to the side and popped my tire. I was scared to tell my dad because my mom had done the same thing a few weeks before. It took some time, but I finally told him, and he was so loving in his response. I'll never forget what that felt like. I had worked myself up so much and was preparing for the worst, yet he said, "It's okay, baby. Accidents happen." I asked him why he wasn't mad at me and just kept apologizing. He reassured me that everyone makes mistakes and it would be okay. He told me I never needed to be afraid to tell him when something happened because he was a safe place for me—that day changed how I approached situations with my parents. It was a pivotal moment for me as a teenager because I had even more confidence that they cared for me more than the mistakes I would make.

When you show your kids that you can be a safe place for them, no matter how big the mistake is - they will come to you. I am naturally a private person and try to deal with things independently. But that doesn't help me in the long run when I need support or

I need you to love me

guidance. I am naturally hard on myself, so I needed someone to be gentle with me and care more about me than what happened. My hesitation was not about them but how I saw the situation and processed the possibilities; their response changed me for the better! My dad has a saying, **"You don't see things the way they are. You see things the way you are."** I needed a mindset shift in that scenario, and I am grateful it happened the way it did.

WHITNEY

There are no perfect parents, but mine were pretty close. Now, as a parent, I use so many of the tools my parents gave me growing up in their household. I was the kid who left things everywhere and spilled everything. We had a lot of "awareness" conversations, but I always felt loved and accepted. I use this as an example because I had a hard time not feeling like "spilling" and "leaving" things were a part of my identity. I still struggle with it.

The conversation went something like this, *"I'm sorry that you left your stuffed animal at the hotel. I have also forgotten things before that mattered to me. Remember, last time we went back to get it, but this time we won't because you really need to work on being responsible for your things if you are going to choose to bring something."*

You can help your child be better, teach them tools for growth, and make them feel accepted for who they are. A lot of parents swing the pendulum and stop correcting their kids because they want them to feel loved and accepted. Or they want their child to stop crying, so they just go back and

> WHEN YOUR KIDS GROW UP, THEY WILL FEEL LOVED AND ACCEPTED IF YOU HAVE CORRECTED THEM IN A LOVING AND REASSURING WAY.

get the stuffed animal instead of using what happened as an opportunity for growth.

When your kids grow up, they will feel loved and accepted if you have corrected them in a loving and reassuring way. They will actually thank you for the correction and direction you gave because it will be a part of the legacy of love you left in their lives. You correct because you love and accept. My parents were masters at this and still are.

APPRECIATION

Dear Parent:

I need your love expressed through your APPRECIATION of me for who I am, your child. Your ability to show appreciation for me will help me learn to appreciate myself. By showing your appreciation for me, for who I am to you, I will not only learn to appreciate myself, but your example will help me learn to appreciate others. Someone has said that "the greatest human need is to feel appreciated." If you cannot appreciate me, I cannot learn to appreciate you. You are my teacher. You are helping to shape my self-image. If I hear from you that I am appreciated, it will go a long way in helping me feel valuable in this life.

To APPRECIATE means *"to value greatly or to be grateful for."* I need to feel that you are grateful for me. I need to feel that you value my existence. Before I can ever truly be grateful for you, I must feel that you are grateful for me.

The first and most important place I will ever feel valuable in my life is when I'm with you. The key to getting what you want in life is to give value to others before you can expect to receive it yourself. I will not learn to be grateful for you because you buy me the best clothes, buy me the most expensive toys, or give me a lot of things. I will learn to value you and others in this life as a result of the value you express to me for who I am. I will never feel truly appreciated by anyone in this world, nor will I ever easily appreciate anyone else, if you never express your appreciation for me.

Your Child

JOSH

When I was a teenager, as my dad and I were driving through a toll-booth (this was before toll tags), he handed some change to the attendant and while doing so said, "God loves you. God has a plan for your life. God wants you to know you are special! God bless you."

I sat there for a while and said, "I don't think I could ever do what you do, because I'm not like you." My dad said, "You don't have to be like me; you need to be you. God made you the way you are on purpose and He just wants you to be the best you that you can be. You have talents, abilities, and skills that I don't have, and the world needs those too."

That conversation remains a positive defining moment for me. Not only is it okay for me to be me, but the "me" that I am is celebrated, valued, and necessary. I needed my dad to tell me that he appreciated me for who I am.

Throughout my life, my parents have been intentional to notice who I am and who I am on the road to becoming. They haven't just appreciated my natural strengths or abilities. They have noticed and celebrated my efforts to develop skills and abilities that aren't natural to me, as well.

One of the greatest things my parents have ever done for me is to make me feel valued and appreciated for the uniqueness of who I am. They've made me feel valuable; not only to the world, but to them as parents and leaders; they've made me feel like there really is something special that only I can bring to our family and by extension to the world itself. It's one of the most significant things that makes me who I am today. I am confident that they believe what makes me different from them makes me great, and I'm not just tolerated, I'm celebrated. Their acceptance of me has shaped my self-image.

If you know me, you know me. There's not a version of me that is different based on the rooms I'm in. I love myself and I am comfortable in my own skin. That is all because of how my parents appreciated me for who I was throughout my life. It laid the foundation for how I see myself. In the midst of my own insecurity, I would frequently think to myself, "If they think I'm great, and they're smarter and wiser than me, they're probably right!" Now, I can celebrate and honor the greatness in those around me - including my wife and children - because of how my parents have helped me to see myself.

KEELA

Throughout my life, my dad has written love letters to me. In them, he would express what greatness he saw in me and tell me how much he loved me. When cellphones came out, he would text me, call me, and even leave voicemails, singing an original song he came up with on the spot; the song was expressing how much he loved me and how special I was to him. My dad was always so intentional with loving me that, growing up, I never sought out love or approval from boys around me. So many girls I grew up with were **boy-crazy**. These girls sought affection and attention from guys who didn't care about them long-term. My dad's efforts towards me were an incredible way to help me understand my value as a woman and know how I should be treated. No one could out-express or out-do my dad, so I never needed that from anyone else. A father plays such a significant role in his daughter's life. His intentionality with her, or the lack thereof, will be something she uses as a rubric for the rest of her life with other men. Several studies have shown that daughters who have close relationships with their fathers are less likely to suffer from depression and anxiety. They also tend to have higher self-esteem, greater confidence, and a better ability to handle stress and emotional challenges.

When I was young, I always said I wanted to marry my dad, and I did not understand how marriage worked then, obviously. But I knew that I wanted to be with someone who loved me and made me feel important and cared for. My dad set the standard; he taught me that romance was not only possible within the confines of a romantic relationship (between a man and a woman) but that you could live a life of romancing others through the way you love them intentionally. Romance has come to mean something that involves romantic feelings, but the word's origin means a story in the style of Rome. Intimacy, on the other hand, is derived from the Latin *intimus*, meaning *"inner or inmost."* To be intimate with another is to have access to and comprehend the qualities that make a person unique or special. In most Romance languages, the root word for intimate refers to a person's interior and inmost quality. Romance happens through you choosing to know what makes a person feel loved and acting on that knowledge. Because I grew up in a family that led with this mindset, I have lived my life knowing that my worth and value come from God first and that I will not waste my time on relationships or alignments that do not align with what I value. I didn't have to seek meaning or acceptance because my family intentionally fostered it.

WHITNEY

More than my parents corrected me... they encouraged me. They told me how beautiful, special, powerful, anointed, gifted, talented, helpful, wanted, and great I was. They always made me feel that they were happy I was around. In fact, my Dad has always called me his "Oxygen". He says anytime I am with or around him, he can breathe better. The other nickname he gave me was "Giggles".

My Dad used to ask all of us, "What do you contribute to this family?" I remember one time I had a hard time answering that question and he said, "Do you know why I call you Giggles? It's because you bring so much joy to our family and to the world." I felt so loved and appreciated by that response. I never had to guess again what I brought into a room. I am like a breath of fresh air and I am a joy bringer. I believe it so much that I put "Giggles"

I need you to love me

on my license plate when I turned 16. Now I bear the honor of striving to bring that into every atmosphere.

When you, as a parent, make your child feel appreciated, it does so much more than encourage them. It helps them discover what they bring to the world and to recognize the power they have that can be appreciated by others.

AFFECTION

Dear Parent:

I need your love expressed to me through your touch: I need your AFFECTION. There is an inner need that each of us possesses—the natural desire to be touched. I need to be held often. I need to feel your hands against mine. I need to feel your arms wrapped around my body. Your embrace gives me much needed security. I need to feel your hands rub through my hair. This makes me feel so special. I need you to kiss me, even though sometimes, I may act like I don't like it. There is nothing in this world that I like better than for you to rub my back, feet, and arms. A good time to do this, by the way, is at night when you put me to bed; but I like it anytime.

AFFECTION is the outward demonstration through your touch of how you feel about me on the inside. AFFECTION is love activated by touch. I will learn the importance of touch by feeling you touch me.

Your Child

JOSH

As of this writing, I'm 36 years old. I have a wife and three children of my own. My wife Courtnei and I have been married for nine years. To this day I still ask my mom to scratch my back. From the time I was little, my dad and I have kissed each other. I can remember being in grade school and middle school, and my dad would walk into my class just to say, "Hey," and he'd give me a kiss in front of all my friends. This wasn't just at school. Every night before I went to bed, he would come in and kiss me goodnight, whether I wanted him to or not.

By the time I got to high school, you'd think this would have ended. However, I began to realize, based on my father's own expression, how important affection was to him, and how important it was to our relationship. So I began to express affection to my dad, kissing him before I left for school, or went to bed. To this day, we kiss.

I understand there might be some hesitation here for you personally. I'm not asking you to do exactly what my parents did. It has never been weird, or inappropriate. My dad has taught me the real value of being loved by a father from the time I was young. I've had a healthy understanding of non-sexual intimacy with those around me because of my parents' affection. I haven't looked for significance, affection, or acceptance from improper, or unhealthy places, because I truly knew how much my parents loved me and showed me affection. Ask yourself how you can show maximum affection to your children.

KEELA

Humans need 8-10 meaningful touches daily; most people never receive that. In our family, we experienced intentional touch and care from both of my parents, and it didn't stop just because we got older. Some people I have talked to say they feel weird about physically loving on their kids once they reach a certain age – but your kids will never stop needing your love. In the early stages of a child's life, the mother usually provides the most physical affection to her children by holding them, rocking them, and soothing them. Because we were constantly loved on physically by both parents, I knew I could go to my mom and ask her to scratch me or sit on my dad's lap at any time.

I will say that when my mom touched me or scratched me, it always made my brain feel like I was on drugs, and it's incredible because research says that there is a unique connection a mother has with their child physically that no one else will ever have. When she touches her child and shows them affection, it releases the same chemicals and hormones as if you were taking drugs. I never saw this intentional love and affection reflected in my friends' families. Now that I am in my 30s, I still feel like I could cuddle up with my mom or dad, and they would respond with the same openness as when I was a little child. Just because your child grows up doesn't mean they stop being your child.

Some moments like this are depicted in shows or movies, but the only time a parent touches their child or grown children is when they are in a severe accident, or they die. At the point an accident or emergency happens, it's too late, and this is typically when people show care and affection. They miss out on intentional connection throughout their life, and at minimum, they give their children a handshake, pat on the back, or side hug. It makes me sad because I know what it feels like to have intimacy with my family. If you desire a relationship with your kids that is not just sweet and connected when they are young, don't stop doing what made you close just because they get older. I want to challenge you to stop thinking it's weird to love on your child; they will never out-grow your love. You are the one person who has the power to create what love and care look like to them. You set the standard for what they will look for in other relationships, which will either be based on what they had or lacked with you.

WHITNEY

One of my greatest memories growing up was that every night for as long as I lived at my parents house, my mom would come into my room. She would talk to me and ask me about my day. As we talked she would scratch my arms and my back. Not only with her words but with her motherly touch, she would help me to open up so we could have a genuine connection.

As an adult, I can tell you that even now that intentional touch from her means so much. Now, my husband scratches my back every night. As a Mom I do the same thing for my children and I ask them if there is anything on their heart they want to talk about, hoping I can make them feel the same way my mom made me feel.

APPROVAL

Dear Parent:

Finally, I need your love expressed to me through your APPROVAL of me for who I am – your child. Your ability to show your approval of me will help me to approve of myself. The necessity for me to approve of myself will help me from having to seek approval from others. This will keep me from much hardship in life. My decisions will not have to be based on the approval of others, and therefore, I will learn to make right decisions regardless of what someone else may think or say. I don't want to go through life trying to please others while making myself miserable in the process.

To APPROVE means to communicate that something is good. I need to feel that I am good. When I do bad things, as all people who are still imperfect invariably do, I do not need to hear how bad I am. You see, I will believe whatever you tell me and act according to your expectations.

When I do something bad, and I will, I need you to discipline me because of the love you have for me and the ability you have to see the good in me, even in a bad situation. I don't need to hear how bad I am, but rather how bad the thing was that I did. I need you to disapprove of my bad actions, not disapprove of me in the process. I need to hear that I am a good child and that good children don't do those bad things.

> I NEED YOU TO DISAPPROVE OF MY BAD ACTIONS, NOT DISAPPROVE OF ME IN THE PROCESS.

I must first believe that I am good before I can understand how bad something is for me. The only reason something should ever be bad for me is because it could keep me from being the good person that you have convinced me that I am.

If you will attempt to strive in these four areas, I will

feel your love always and never have to look elsewhere for love.

A lot of times people say they love you and maybe they really do. But I hope after reading my letter to you, that you will know how to best express your love for me. I promise if you will do these four things for me in expressing your love, it will teach me how to express my love for you. It will also help me to be a secure, well-rounded person in life.

Remember, I love you, not for what you will ever do materially for me, but I love you for who you are – my Parent. I ACCEPT, APPRECIATE, will be AFFECTIONATE, AND APPROVE of you.

Your Child

JOSH

My dad and I couldn't be more opposite. He's a gifted athlete, consistent in the gym, and maintains an inspiring level of discipline to this day. I'm working on that, but haven't had nearly the level of discipline and consistency he has shown throughout his life. He loves people, he's fun, he's highly entertaining, and has a huge personality. Conversely, I quit basketball in high school to focus on being on the student council. I am an introvert with a few close friends and "doing nothing" is my favorite pastime.

Due to my dad's natural preferences, the potential for him to disapprove of me is highly expected based on typical parenting. My preferences often aren't his, and his frequently are not mine. When I quit basketball, he wasn't "disappointed" in me.

I need you to love me

We talked through what I saw as the pros and cons and he did not seem to be upset by my decision as long as I was making it for the right reasons.

One of the greatest predictors of our sense of significance is the approval of those we respect. Children understand themselves to be significant based on the approval of their parents. So often, our greatest issues in life come from a desire for approval and significance that we never experienced at home. Many of the adults we see continually struggling for significance in their life usually have an approval wound that happened in their home growing up.

Unfortunately, most children only experience approval when they win first place, or when they do something the parent sees as worthwhile. What we - your children - need is approval and a sense of significance, even when you may see our achievement as unimportant or unworthy to you personally.

Most people, children, or otherwise, cannot separate their identity from what they do or what they create. So when what they do is criticized, they feel personally insignificant.

Saying, "I'm proud of your hard work" even if your child came in last place, is so much better than saying, "If you're not first, you're last." It's not about giving everyone a medal, and it is not weak parenting to celebrate your children's effort, even if they didn't reach an arbitrary standard.

The greatest thing my parents did to make me feel approved by them was to celebrate my effort, not my achievement. It wasn't always about making an "A" or winning the gold medal. It also certainly wasn't about succeeding in the same places they succeeded. It was about acknowledging my best efforts towards what I was passionate about and championing me all the way.

KEELA

Care plays a significant role in your child's feelings of approval. When you care about something or someone, you put effort towards them. My dad and mom would express what they liked about my unique ways or find ways to get involved with what I was passionate about. My dad would say, if you love it, I love it. It made me feel like he cared about what I cared about and that I was accepted and approved of. When you show approval to your child, it builds up their sense of value, and eventually, they become confident enough and won't need outside approval because they can approve of themselves.

When I was a sophomore in high school, I wanted a pug. We had grown up with pugs, and I missed having one. My dad said if I could find one (for a specific price), he would let me get it. The price point was practically impossible, but I found one in the "Thrifty Nickel" classifieds section. I went to look at the dog with my mom and instantly fell in love with a specific puppy. I asked them to put a ribbon on her so she wouldn't get sold. A few weeks later, my dad called me to come downstairs. I looked down at him and almost missed that he was holding the pug I wanted in his arms. He had gotten her for me! He gave me a card and wrote that he bought her to show me that God knows the desires of our hearts and that he wanted her to always represent that to me in life. Paris, the pug, lived for 14 years and was always such a gift from God. From the time I was 15 until I was 29, she was with me. She was that reminder to me through my ups and downs in high school and even through my divorce at 26. I will never forget that lesson because while not everything has been good, God has always been good and showed up for me in all my seasons. This lesson all stemmed from the fact that my parents didn't have to approve of what I wanted or expressed in that season of life, but they did, and for me, the lesson has transcended decades.

The fact is, you may not be able to approve of everything your child wants or does, and they may even live a lifestyle you cannot support as they get older based on your values. But you can show them approval by loving them simply as your child and always speaking the truth, without having to approve what they do. People minimize how important being approved of as a child is and how it plays a massive role in whether we seek approval as adults. What I have evaluated with friends who have struggled with identity or self-worth is that they did not feel approved of early on in life within their family. They faced abuse or a dismissive or absent parent, which contributed to them seeking out approval from crowds that they never should have been associated with. Approval becomes a much bigger issue if you do not get intentional about it with your kids while they are young. This doesn't mean you do or give them everything they want. Approval is caring about the unique ways that God made them and speaking into that and taking the time to be a prophet in their life and a representation of the heart of God towards them.

WHITNEY

I remember being at a gas station and I asked my mom if I could get a peppermint pattie. She said I could not, but I took them anyway and put them in my back pockets. I got in the very back of the car where no one could see me eat the stolen candy. When I reached in my back pockets, they had melted. I decided to eat one anyway and the melted chocolate was smeared all over my face. I asked my sister to hand me tissues to wipe my mouth and after she handed them to me, she looked back to find my face covered in sticky melted mint chocolate with tissues stuck to it. She realized I had stolen the chocolate and told my parents in the front seat. I was devastated and all the guilt hit me.

After getting a lesson from my Dad on who we are and who we are not, while affirming his belief in who he knew I was... my dad turned the car around and said, "Now we are going to go an hour back to that gas station and you are going to apologize. This will add two hours to our trip but I want you to remember this forever so it never happens again."

Going back and having to apologize was embarrassing and humbling. Not once did my parents make me feel like I was a bad person or tell me they were disappointed in me. They knew their job as my parents was not to focus on the bad I did but to affirm who I am, who God created me to be, and who we chose to be as a family. Their job was to correct and not approve of my behavior.

> YOU CAN CHOOSE NOT TO APPROVE BEHAVIOR WHILE STILL DEEPLY APPROVING OF WHO YOU KNOW YOUR CHILD IS.

You can choose not to approve behavior while still deeply approving of who you know your child is. These are two different things. Even in my worst moments, having parents who corrected me and approved of me made me want to be more for God and to be a great representative of my family.

AN UNLOVELY PLACE

Dear Parent:

For the first nine months of my life, everything seemed fine, I was so close to your heart that I could feel your heartbeat. I could not see you, but I didn't have to, because I could feel you. This was such a LOVELY PLACE.

I was never hungry. I was never thirsty. I was never cold. I was always so comfortable. The temperature was always perfect. I could feel you moving around and I was always so happy because everywhere you went, you took me with you. I didn't really understand where I was. I just knew I was with you and that's all that mattered. This was such a LOVELY PLACE.

I remember hearing your voice. I felt like you were talking just to me. We spent so many special moments together, night and day. Oh, to be totally content. I know what it feels like to be totally content. This was such a LOVELY PLACE.

I could always tell when your hand was on me. I couldn't see it, but its warmth and pulse were indescribable. I would move my hands and my feet to try to touch you. This was such a LOVELY PLACE.

Then came a day, I will never forget. I felt you were very uncomfortable and it made me uncomfortable. You were breathing very hard and I could tell you were in pain. I began to feel myself being pushed against and there was nothing I could do about it. I could tell something was happening, but I did not understand. This LOVELY PLACE I had known for so long, was now becoming very uncomfortable. I began to feel very cold and I could hear strange voices all around me.

Then the worst thing that has ever happened to me happened. As I felt you pushing against me, I felt some strange cold fingers wrap themselves around my head and begin to pull on me. While you pushed, they pulled. I didn't understand what was happening to me. I could not breathe. I was getting colder and colder.

Then all of the sudden, I did not feel you anymore. Something else was holding me. Where was my LOVELY PLACE? I wanted it back. I wanted you back. I began to cry. What was this place? What was this unlovely place?

Then came the final shock. Something cold and sharp permanently separated us. I was cold. I was hungry. I was uncomfortable. I was alone. What was this unlovely place?

I know now. It's THE WORLD. I NEED YOU TO LOVE ME, because the world is an unlovely place.

Your Child

I need you to love me

2

Please be a good example

I need someone to follow.

Dear Parent:

There is a truism that says, *"Lead, follow, or get out of the way."* In this world that we live in, there must be leaders, and there must be followers. At this point in my life, I need you to be my leader. I need someone that loves me enough to show me what is right and what is wrong; what is acceptable and what is unacceptable; what is best and what is second best. But I need you to show me first, not tell me. Because an ounce of example is worth a ton of teaching.

I need someone to lead me that has no hidden agendas, or something to gain by me following where they want me to go, or doing what they want me to do. I need someone to lead me who has my best interest in mind, because they love me and want the best for me.

I need someone to lead me that I can trust with my success and my failures. I need someone who will lead me and evaluate me based on who I am becoming in the process, not by what I am achieving along the way. I need a leader who knows me better than I know myself, and who can keep me from making some of the same mistakes they have made in this unlovely place.

I need someone who will lead me by their example; someone I can learn from their failures how not to do things; and learn from their successes, how to win.

What I don't need is for someone to say, "Do as I say, and not as I do". As your child, the way I understand it, whatever is good for you, is going to be good for me. Whatever is bad for you, is going to be bad for me. Regardless of what you might say, your actions will always speak to me louder than your words. I will do what you say only if I see you live what you say. I will only have a conflict with you if you play by a different set of rules than you assign to me.

Please don't misunderstand me. I want to do what you say, because the only real goal in life I have right now is to please you. I really want to do the right thing, but I need you to lead me the right way. I need a leader who will lead by example. I need someone to lead me where I have never been before and where I could never go if no one led me.

A good leader has the ability to help people become what they would not, and to do what they could not, if it had not been for that leader. I need you to help me become the person that I could never become without you. I need you to help me accomplish things I could never accomplish if it had not been for your leadership, your example in my life.

> A GOOD LEADER HAS THE ABILITY TO HELP PEOPLE BECOME WHAT THEY WOULD NOT, AND TO DO WHAT THEY COULD NOT, IF IT HAD NOT BEEN FOR THAT LEADER.

I am counting on you to help me. I will never be all I could have been without your help. I promise, I will be and I will do, whatever you show me by your example.

I know this: If you're too big to follow, you're too small to lead. If I ever am going to be a leader someday, I need to learn how to follow a leader. I will be as good or bad as you are.

Please be a good example, because your life shows me what is possible.

Your Child.

JOSH

Great parents have a special ability. They have the ability to see who their kids are becoming, and separate that from how they are currently behaving. In my house, my parents were first and foremost our leaders. The quote we heard often was "you don't have to like me, but you will respect me."

My parents wanted us to be friends; they wanted us to have a great relationship; but they saw their role in my life as greater than the role of a "friend." They were mentors, life coaches, the first people who ever gave me any kind of example to follow. They were the God-given stewards of my destiny.

That's a pretty big responsibility, but they loved me enough to live the values that they wanted me to live. My Dad taught me a great lesson about parenting early in my childhood: *"What you do in moderation, your followers will do in excess."* If we have attitude issues, disrespect, anger, or lack discipline, how can we ever expect anyone around us to be any different?

There were three things I was strongly disciplined for as a child:
1) Bad Attitude/Disrespecting other people
2) Lying
3) Disrespecting My Mom

As far back as I can remember, my parents tried hard not to put their struggles on display for us as their children. If they did, they apologized to us and told us they didn't want to lead us that way. I've never seen either one of my parents lie or deceive anyone; and in our home, my mom was cherished and honored because that was the way my Dad treated her. My parents worked hard on their attitude and have always treated people around them with respect. And they took responsibility when they didn't.

> "WHAT YOU DO IN MODERATION, YOUR FOLLOWERS WILL DO IN EXCESS."

My parents could discipline me in these things because they sought to live them first. It doesn't mean they were perfect. Parenting children doesn't mean you're perfecting them, it means you're leading from the front. My parents made the decision to show us what following their example looked like by following it themselves.

Plutarch said this: "For the one who is tripping over cannot straighten up someone else, nor can the ignorant person teach, the disorderly establish order, the disorganized organize, the ungoverned govern."

The problem with bad parents is not that they don't have the knowledge, it is that they do not apply what they know. If you are not striving to be great yourself, your children have little hope of being great. If you are not positive, your children will not be positive. If you are angry, your children will be angry. If you are held back by your insecurity and fear, your children will be too. The only way for your children to have a chance to overcome is if you overcome first, and create a path for them to follow.

Remember you are the first model of anything for your kids. The model of thinking, being (attitude), and doing (action). Be the kind of person you want your kids to grow up to be. They will end up being like you anyway. If you model it, your children will always believe it is possible for them. If you are great, your children will be great in their own right.

As I was growing up, we had a family mission statement; "Never allow the good to be the robber of the best."

My parents lived this first. As they raised us, they began to talk to us about living life according to core values. This is the most important thing about being someone worth following: understanding your and your family's virtue, your core values, and your true north.

Please be a good example

As these things were shaped in my childhood, my parents discussed with us what it meant to follow them. There are five core values in the Craft family. We call these the **"Big Five"**:

1) Honor
2) Positive Attitude
3) Excellence
4) Generosity
5) Personal Leadership

My parents lived these things intentionally. And as we got older, they began to communicate to us that living these five things was what it meant to be a "Craft." In my 20's, my dad sat all of us down together and said, "There's a lot of things you can follow me in, but if you want to follow me and your mom, follow us in these things."

When I got married in 2014, my dad and I sat down together and designed a family crest together that embodies these things. These are the values that I am modeling and will teach to my children as they get older. On this crest, there's four unique elements. The crown represents honor. The heart signifies a positive attitude. The book stands for excellence, and the tree stands for generosity. When these four unique pieces come together, they form the crest which is the standard we lead ourselves to personally.

My parents were not and are not perfect, but they instilled in me such a strong desire to "live like them" that I have this crest and our family mission statement tattooed on my arm.

"Never allow good to be robber of the best."

KEELA

One of the things that inspires me about both of my parents is that they are authentically who they are, no matter what. They are genuine about what they say and how they live. I have never seen them talk about or say something they were not striving for personally. My mom and dad led us by example, and they would say things like, ***"We chose to do this in our life, and you are going to have to decide what kind of person you want to be."*** This challenged me to be my best, even when they weren't watching, because of the person I decided I wanted to be. Most of my friends' parents would tell them not to do things they were doing, and they did not lead by example.

You cannot expect your kids to be any better than you if you do not discipline yourself or push yourself to be better as their parents. My parents didn't just tell us what to do; they led us through action. So often, people talk about how they will never be like their mom or dad because their parents were not great examples. People can get so focused on how they don't want to be that they become even worse than their parents. While you cannot control what others do or say, you can always choose what you magnify. If you don't have the best example and you magnify it, that's what you'll get more of.

On the other hand, if you think about, talk about, and focus on positive outcomes, things can get better. I would have struggled if my parents had said one thing and did another, but sadly, this is a reality for many people when it comes to their parents. It built so much confidence in me to see the fruit in my parents' lives. I knew if they said something, they were striving to be and do that in their lives. No parent is perfect, and I do not think it is healthy to put pressure on yourself to be perfect. But you can be someone who strives to be great and lives a life worth following.

Please be a good example

> WHILE YOU CANNOT CONTROL WHAT OTHERS DO OR SAY, YOU CAN ALWAYS CHOOSE WHAT YOU MAGNIFY.

My parent's example led me to want to be a person that lived up to my word. I wanted to be someone that others could count on and depend on. I saw the value in this because of the environment I was raised in and the example I had at home. I remember my parents teaching us how to have healthy conflict resolution, and while it didn't happen often, when my parents fought in front of us, they made sure to make up in front of us. We didn't just see the issues or the intensity, but we also saw the love and care they showed each other, which, as a kid, significantly helped develop how I could approach conflict in the future. Your kids don't need your perfect, polished example. They need to know the realness of the struggle and how you overcame it. What inspired me the most was not that my parents handled everything perfectly but that they shared their struggles and overcame them.

WHITNEY

Growing up, I went to a private Christian School and there were a lot of Pastor's kids and high-level leader's kids at my school. It seemed like most of these kids had parents a lot like mine. I had a hard time figuring out why so many people I was around were dysfunctional. Many of them were depressed, anxious, and severely rebellious.

One day I noticed my classmate, who had a very high-profile Pastor as a father, was very upset. He was clearly struggling and not in a good place. I went over to him and asked what was wrong and if he was okay. He said, "Well you know what it's like... seeing your parents on stage telling everyone how to have a great marriage, a great family, great kids, and a great ministry. Then they come home and that is not the story of your life. They scream, yell, and I feel like they hate me. They are both so fake. You know what I mean?"

I had no idea what to say because I honestly had no idea what he meant. I have parents that showed followable excellence in every area of their lives. I felt deeply loved and I wanted to be like them. I saw them not only living what they preached but they were open and honest about when it was more difficult. This in turn made me feel like I didn't have to be perfect... I just had to do my best.

I remember making a "C" on a math test and I was so upset about it. I came home crying and my dad asked me if I did my best. I truly did. I studied hard and I went to a tutor before and after school. He said, "If you did your best then I am proud of you and you should be proud of that grade. I don't care if you get "A's." I care that you do your best and only you can measure if you did."

Peace just washed over me. Not because my Dad wasn't mad but because I knew I had parents who weren't perfect and were not asking me to be. They were striving to be their best and just asking me to do the same. I couldn't live up to perfection but I could TOTALLY work to be my best, just like they were.

Your kids need to see you living what you say, but they also need to see you being real about how it's not always easy. It humanizes you and lets them know that they are not weak or damaged but they are just like you. And just like you, we are striving together to be our best.

TEACH ME ABOUT GOD

Dear Parent:
The greatest thing you can ever do for me, is to teach me about God. There are so many questions that I have about life.

Who made the earth, the skies and the trees?
Who made the birds and the deep blue seas?
Who made the stars that shine bright above?
Who made the wind underneath the wings of a dove?

How did I get here, I'm not really sure?
How does the air I'm breathing stay pure?
How do my fingers move when I want them to?
How does the rain know when to get through?

Why does it get hot, and why does it get cold?
Why do people like you look so old?
Why am I here, does anyone know?
Why is it always time to go?

Where did I come from to get here?
Where did I learn how to fear?
Where am I headed, am I in a place?
Where do I fit in this lonely place?
When will I know I'm where I'm supposed to be?
When will I know I'm truly free?
When will I find what I'm looking for?
When will I know I've walked through the right door?

What's really important in this life I now live?
What should I take or what should I give?

What is my purpose; someone show me the way?
What will I become, by the end of this day?

Your Child

JOSH

The greatest gift my parents gave me is the gift of a relationship with Jesus Christ. Understanding that God has a plan for my life, that he sent His son Jesus to die on a cross long before I existed because of His love for me, has been the most extraordinary discovery. My parents have loved me, accepted me, and told me how great I can be, and they've introduced me to the person who put all of that potential inside of me.

Think about this, the relationship your children have with you will show them the kind of relationship God has with them. Your child's relationship with you will be their model for their relationship with God. If you are angry at your kids when they make a mistake, you teach them that God is angry. If you are indifferent to your kids when they are successful, they will think God is too. If you don't believe that your kids can win, they will think that God doesn't think they can win either. God has given you His children to raise and teach about Him, because He wants to leave a great legacy through your family.

Teach your children grace, love, and acceptance. Teach them to treat people like Jesus did. Teach your children to have great dreams and to believe in God and have confidence in the gifts that He has given them. Teach them that God has plans to prosper them, and that Jesus came to give them an abundant life.

Please be a good example

Put their life in an eternal perspective. Let them know that even when they are afraid, insecure, in distress, and surrounded on every side, there is a God who fights for them, who believes in them even when they don't believe in themselves. A God who can do anything. A God who saw them and knew them before they were born and called them according to His purpose to do great works. Teach them this by being that way towards them.

From the time I was very small, every time I prayed with my Dad we kneeled. We would kneel by my bed or my parents' bed, and my parents also had a prayer room in our house where we would go together to pray. We did this up until the time I moved into my own house.

We didn't just pray, worship, and attend church. I watched my parents. I watched how they treated people with grace and mercy. I've watched as they have transformed and grown in their own walk with God.

Most families don't do this—that's something you would see in a Norman Rockwell painting. Families should do this, not because it makes you more spiritual, but it shows your children what it's like to honor and esteem God. It shows your children how much you love your Father in heaven, and teaches them to do the same.

I have a great relationship with God today, and know He loves me deeply because my parents did the same. I am committed to building the Kingdom of God through my life because my parents did the same. I don't have "church hurt" and I'm not mad at God when bad things happen, because my parents walked through the same stuff. I am deeply devoted to submitting myself to God and His plans for my life, because I saw my parents do that. At the same time, I watched it work. I saw God move in their lives. I saw Him show up when they took steps of faith. I have watched God prosper them in every way, not just financially.

KEELA

I saw my mom and dad pursue and develop a personal relationship with God. The way they did that was unique to each of them, but we never had a season where God was not at the forefront of our family. We never ate a meal without praying. When we got hurt, they would pray for us. When we were scared, they would pray for us. My parents also taught us to talk to God personally. They didn't speak to God for us; they had us actively participate in spiritual things. Most families do not talk about God or intentionally interact with Him as a family. More often, these families come to church occasionally or only during the holidays, and they think that attending church twice a year is how you have a relationship with Jesus. Therefore, their kids do not prioritize an intimate or intentional relationship with God. I always respected that my parents didn't act like they had all the answers or knew everything about God. When I would ask them about something they were unsure of, they would simply say, *"I'm not sure, but we can ask God about that."* I never felt like questioning things was off-limits. It is rare in a Christian household to encourage your kids to question, but I believe you learn most by asking questions.

We must address why we feel uncomfortable when our kids ask us things that we aren't sure about, especially regarding God. I am sure it would be nice to have all the answers, but there are things that we will never know until we go to Heaven. My parents made me feel that it was okay to ask questions and did not shut me down for asking. They also taught me it was okay if I didn't always know the answer. I think people shy away from encouraging

Please be a good example

questions about God or being the example spiritually for their kids because they have not been consistent in their relationship; they probably have little intimacy with God themselves. I was inspired by my parents' relationship with God, and I could watch what they did and apply it. My approach or style may be different, but I could learn from their intentionality and discipline. My parents were a fantastic example of this because their relationship with God was out in the open; it was the foundation of their lives and our family, as it should be. Therefore, my relationship with God was never just through my parents. I learned how to connect to God myself and make my own decision to follow Him because they showed me how.

WHITNEY

I think it's easy to forget that as the parent you are the primary faith trainer. Many times, we rely on the church to teach our kids to worship, read scripture, and know the stories of the Bible. That really is our responsibility. Our kids' faith and giving them the foundation to walk it out in their lives is up to us.

As kids we were constantly in church but I really don't remember kids' church teaching me much about the Bible. Church was a community and where my friends were. When I was 9 years old my parents started the church and it became about serving other families and being a part of their walk with Jesus. I knew and saw my parents deeply loving God. The church was the overflow of what was happening in private. My Dad

> CHURCH IS A PART OF OUR RHYTHM OF LIFE, OUR COMMUNITY, AND AIDS US IN OUR WALK WITH GOD. JUST GOING TO CHURCH DOES NOT MAKE YOU A FOLLOWER OF JESUS.

constantly played worship music in our home. I have core memories of my mom and dad working out to LOUD worship music as I worshiped and danced around them. Not only did this foster my love for worship but my love for Jesus. I experienced His presence early in my home and I knew He was real because my parents set the atmosphere for it.

I wanted more of God from an early age as I watched them read their Bibles and tie every lesson they taught me back to The Word. Your children don't just need to be told Jesus is real... they need to experience for themselves that He is. You can set those atmospheres and show them that not only is He real in your life but He can be real in theirs. Church is a part of our rhythm of life, our community, and aids us in our walk with God. Just going to church does not make you a follower of Jesus.

TEACH ME ABOUT AUTHORITY

Dear Parent:
Authority is defined as *"the power or right to give orders and make others obey."* I have wondered exactly what it is that gives another person the right to have authority over someone else. At this point in my life, the simple conclusion that I have drawn is this: YOU have given me life, so YOU must know what is best for me. Therefore, I will do whatever you say as my authority.

However, it will not take me long to adopt your perception of authority based on your perspective of authority. You see, YOU are my leader, the example I will follow. Whatever your perception; whatever your perspective, spoken or unspoken, it will become my

Please be a good example

> WHATEVER YOUR PERCEPTION; WHATEVER YOUR PERSPECTIVE, SPOKEN OR UNSPOKEN, IT WILL BECOME MY PHILOSOPHY.

philosophy. I am seeing authority through your eyes. I am hearing authority through your lips. I am developing my philosophy of life, based not on just what I see and hear, but also based on your actions.

Let me explain:

A. How you see God is how I see God.

If God is your final authority and everything you do is based on what He says, then eventually I will realize a few important things about you.

1. You don't know everything there is to know, and you need help too, from time to time.

2. By acknowledging God as your final authority, I will be able to see that you want the best for yourself, based on what God wants for you. This will help me understand that because you want what God wants for you, then that means you want what God wants for me too. I will never have trouble following someone who I know is following "The Final Authority." There may be times in my life where I resist, but take comfort; you have resisted before also. If you will lead me in the paths of righteousness for His name's sake,

I promise you, I will eventually get to where He wants me. Your labor will not be in vain.

B. How you see government officials, the President, elected officials, and your local police will be how I see them.

Your attitude towards these people will not only reflect your view, but will greatly affect mine. You really need to understand that I am watching you all the time. Your perception of these people will directly affect my perception of you. Your attitude towards them will influence my attitude towards you.

C. How you see the Church, will be the way I see the Church.

If you talk negatively about a Pastor, I won't believe in him, and I won't believe in you either. If you criticize the Church, I will not want to go to church. If you talk critically about people in the Church, I will be critical and negative also. If you say the church has hurt you and that's why you don't go, I'll get hurt and do the same thing.

Remember, you are my teacher. You are my example. I will see what you see. I will hear what you hear. I will do whatever you do. I will submit (to yield oneself to the authority of another) to you, as you submit to those who are in authority over you. Your attitude towards authority will be reflected in my attitude towards you. Someone has said, "What you sow is what you reap." I will be your constant reminder that this universal principle is true. I am the seed you have produced on this earth. I haven't experienced what you have in life yet, and perhaps, I never will, but one thing is for sure: I am and will be the result of how you responded or reacted to what you have gone through.

Your Child

JOSH

ROMANS 13 says that all authority that exists comes from God. The primary way God tests us in life is in our relationship with authority. Primarily Him. Think about the Garden of Eden; the sin of Adam and Eve wasn't eating from the tree; it was disobeying God as their authority.

Original sin was humanity's inability to properly honor authority. Now, think about today, the Bible clearly commands us to tithe as an honor issue with God. It actually commands us to give God the first 10% of all of our increase. Statistically, only 9% of Christians actually do this. There may be a lot of reasons and excuses, but 91% of Christians live in constant disobedience to God, specifically in the area of finances.

I believe that God tests us through how we choose to honor authority, because honor is always a choice. The way you choose to honor authority is many times the way your children will choose to honor you. How can we be an authority when we ourselves don't honor authority? If you are not submitted to authority, how can you expect your children to submit to you?

Most people (91%) can't submit to God's authority, so how many people are really submitted to their earthly authorities at work, at church, or in society? If we believe God's word, then we must believe the words of Romans 13, that God places all authority–good or bad, right or wrong. This doesn't mean that it's easy to honor authority, but we do it because we are supposed to teach others.

Ultimately, with our kids, the way we honor earthly authority is going to be how our children learn to honor God. When I was a child, there wasn't a distinction between my parents and God. Not that I saw my parents as God; but having a concept of God and honoring Him starts with how we honor people.

> ...THE WAY WE HONOR EARTHLY AUTHORITY IS GOING TO BE HOW OUR CHILDREN LEARN TO HONOR GOD.

My Dad has been someone's boss since his mid-twenties. While he was raising me, he could have raised me with a "boss" mentality. He and my Mom could have met with all my teachers when I had a problem, and blamed it on them. They could have left churches, businesses, and relationships like most people do when things become uncomfortable. But they didn't. From a young age, I was taught that we always honor.

The only things that you or I can control in life are our thoughts, attitudes, and actions. Nothing else. Honor is always an appropriate thought, attitude, and action. It was one of the "Big Five" (core values) in our house growing up. My parents used this philosophy with us while we were being raised, and now, no matter what situation I am in, I seek to honor. At the DMV, being pulled over

Please be a good example

for speeding, working with elders, whatever the situation, I have been trained that my response should be honor.

That means that even if I'm leaving a relationship, I don't talk negatively about someone or bad- mouth them. I do what I feel like I need to do, while maintaining honor, even if that person is talking negatively about me. I've watched my parents model that too. There are people, to this day, who are poisonous in what they say about my parents to me and to others, but I've never - to my knowledge - heard my parents say or do anything that dishonors that person.

Walking in honor would not be possible for me if my parents had not lived this way. But, because they modeled honor and authority, I get to do the same thing.

KEELA

One of the most vulnerable things about being a parent is that while you are an authority, you cannot force or make anyone obey you; they still have a choice to follow you or not. Some kids realize this earlier than others, but your kids will learn how to treat authority by how you approach it. Think about how you treat the things of God, your spouse, and those in leadership above you – your kids are watching how you honor those people in your life as an authority. Honor is a massive lesson regarding authority that we all will face, but honor is not a blanket commandment for every leader in your life. You can choose who you submit to and who you honor; your kids are no different. They will decide whether to submit and honor you at a certain point.

My dad led the way when it came to honor within our family. I saw him honor my mom and honor us as his family. I saw my dad honor people who did not deserve it, and honestly, it sometimes confused me. I recall a specific instance where someone spread negative things about him to anyone who would listen, and I asked him how he felt about it. You don't lose the ability to feel just because you become a parent, but very few parents share their internal emotional journey in situations like that with their kids. My dad never spoke negatively about this person; when I asked him about it, he told me it hurt. He explained to me that **"hurt people, hurt people."** He grabbed my hands and said, *"Let's pray for them; you never know what they are going through."* I remember opening my eyes as my dad prayed; I watched him with conviction ask God to speak to them and bless them. I was amazed; what happened next was unbelievable, and it wasn't the only time it happened; he wrote them a check.

I was blown away and asked him why he would do that. He told me that while this person was not honorable, he would not let the situation cause him to be dishonorable, and if there was anything in his heart that he was still struggling with, blessing them was what he wanted his response to be. He taught me that the devil wants us to curse our enemies, but God says to bless them. MATTHEW 5:43–44 says, "YOU HAVE HEARD THAT IT WAS SAID, 'YOU SHALL LOVE YOUR NEIGHBOR AND HATE YOUR ENEMY.' BUT I SAY TO YOU, LOVE YOUR ENEMIES, BLESS THOSE WHO CURSE YOU, DO GOOD TO THOSE WHO HATE YOU, AND PRAY FOR THOSE WHO SPITEFULLY USE YOU AND PERSECUTE YOU." I saw my dad live that out in action, and I don't care how mature or incredible you are; honoring someone when they have dishonored you is not easy. But when you have the power of God - it is possible. In the Bible, honoring your parents is the only commandment that comes with a promise at the end of it. It says in Exodus 20:12 that when you honor your

Please be a good example

parents, you will have a long life. I believe that this means it can go the other way.

You may not think teaching your kids to honor is essential, but by helping them understand honor, you can release a promise from God in their lives. When children are young and living at home, it is clear what it means to honor their parents. You can receive this promise anytime with your parents, even as an adult. The promise from God listed in Exodus is for everyone who applies the principle of honoring. But to be clear, honor does not always mean obedience or submission. The basic idea of the Hebrew word translated as **"honor"** here is *to give weight to*, and your parents have weight because of the position they hold in your life: you wouldn't be here without them. Honoring your father and mother is central to being in and living outside of God's covenant. This same perspective is reflected in Proverbs with the many appeals to follow the instruction of your mother and father because the ideal is that they impart the wisdom of God. However, Paul in Ephesians 6 qualifies this command to say, honor your parents if they live up to the ideal of godly, wise parents. Overall, I have learned that honor reflects the type of person you want to be; it is not based on what another person does or doesn't do.

WHITNEY

When we were young, we had a singing group called *"Two Sisters & A Bro."* There was a song called "Heavenly Father" that my dad wrote to teach us and others who to pray for and how to pray. My parents called the prayer in the song ***"The 5 Finger Prayer."***

The thumb was prayer for our friends and family. The pointer was to pray for the people who don't know Jesus. The middle finger was to pray for those in authority over us. The ring finger is to pray for the homeless and sick people in the hospital and our pinky is when we pray for ourselves. First of all, I know my parents taught us to have the fear of the Lord. As parents they modeled the importance of prayer and obedience.

> CHOOSING TO DISHONOR WILL ONLY HARM ME, BUT CHOOSING TO HONOR GOD, TRUST HIM, AND PRAY ABOUT EVERYTHING SHOWS MY RESPECT FOR WHO HE HAS PUT IN PLACE AND ULTIMATELY MY RESPECT FOR HIM.

I love that the middle finger in the 5 finger prayer signifies those who are in authority over us because in our society that is the finger that is used to show dishonor and disrespect to others. When I look at my fingers, I see the 5 finger prayer that reminds me not only to honor God with my hands, but that every finger represents something I am surrendering to Him. I don't have to show dishonor because I know, even when I disagree, there is a lot more power in my prayer to overcome any attitude of dishonor. Choosing to dishonor will only harm me, but choosing to honor God, trust Him, and pray about everything shows my respect for who He has put in place and ultimately my respect for Him.

A great tool for teaching your children to honor authorities is to teach them to pray about everything just like the Bible says. Fearing God, trusting God, and submitting everything to Him enables you to show honor to others and to God. When you struggle with your boss, let your children see you pray for them. When you struggle with the political climate, let your children see you pray about it. When you are mad because your kid's teacher did not act right, show your kids how to respond by prayer. Let them see and hear you pray; then lead them to do the same.

Please be a good example

TEACH ME ABOUT RESPECT

Dear Parent:
Respect is defined as *"admiration felt towards a person or thing that has good qualities or achievement; to be considerate."* I need to be taught to respect God, others, myself, and things, including money. I cannot overemphasize this fact enough: I will learn this from you. I will learn to respect or to disrespect, by taking note of what you value. What I value, I will respect.

Someone has said that you always need to respect elders. Why? Is it just because they are older? Does older mean wiser? Should I respect someone because they are wiser than me? Should I respect them because they are a human life that God has created?

I really want you to know how I will learn respect: I will learn to respect you, God and others when I feel respected, not for the things I do, but for who I am, YOUR CHILD. I will learn to value myself when I feel that you value me. What I value, I will respect.

I need you to teach me about money, the value of money. I need to understand how important it is to give to God and to other people in need. If I can learn at an early age, to consider God and others before myself, without being put down in the process, I believe I can be a success in life.

Who and what you consider and respect, will be the values in life on which I will place a premium. I am watching you. As you show me respect and what to respect, I will learn to respect.

Your Child

JOSH

First, on money. All throughout my life, my dad has had a financial philosophy. He's never been in debt outside of his house payment. He has 22 different rules for money that he taught me. He taught me the **70-10-10-10 principle**. 70% of your income is discretionary. 10% is your tithe, 10% is your over and above giving, 10% goes to savings. He also taught me what to do with the 70%.

Keith Craft's Financial Philosophy

1) First Fruit is returned to God
   - First 10%

2) Be a Kingdom Builder/Advancer
   - Second 10% - Over and Above Giving

3) Bills
   - Seek to only have bills that are affordable after you put God first and give over and above.

4) Short term savings
   - Ideally 3-6 months of bills. If you don't have short term savings, save 10% of your income until you have short term savings. After you build your savings, invest that 10% towards retirement.

Please be a good example

5) **Retirement**
    - Third 10% - Never to be touched for any reason until retirement. Invest this money so that you can live comfortably after you're done working

6) **Investing**
    - Invest this money in more risky and speculative things that can potentially make you a larger return. Only invest money that you can afford to lose.

7) **Toys**
    - Toys are anything that you do for fun. Boats, Fun cars, second homes, vacations, entertainment, etc. should never be bills that require you to make a payment.

8) **Reduce debt along the way.**
    - This means paying extra amounts every month towards debt while doing the other 7 things.

I know this financial philosophy works, because it's worked in his life, and it's worked in my life. It made him a millionaire by 40. It made me a millionaire by the time I turned 35. For most of my 20's and 30's, my household income was below six figures. I tithed on my first paycheck at 16. I've never had debt, always made payments on time, and I attribute my personal financial success to following my dad's proven philosophy.

Also, respect isn't just our treatment of authority or money. It relates to how we treat everyone, including ourselves. Respect for others will stem from our respect for ourselves.

One of the greatest things I've seen my parents teach is the value of every person's "1%." 99% of human DNA is the same, there is only a 1% difference between you and me, and everyone else who has been born, or everyone that ever will be born. My dad wrote a book about it, called **Your Divine Fingerprint**.

Our 1% is the unique deposit of God's glory in each one of us. Every person alive today, every person who has ever been alive, or ever will be alive is created in God's image. That means all people (including you and me) are worthy of respect, because we all have a part of God in us.

At base level, I can respect myself because there is a part of me that is more than human. There is a part of me that is the image of God. My parents taught me that. Well, they didn't just teach me. They showed me.

I had an English teacher my freshman year of high school that I was convinced had it out for me. To this day, I still think that's true. I have never been treated the way I was treated by her before or since. Of course, there was nothing wrong with me. 15-year old, immature me was not the issue; this teacher had just decided to single me out and treat me unfairly. At least, that was what I told myself. If I'm honest, 20 years later, I still feel that way.

There was one particular exchange this teacher and I had where she said I needed to respect her. I responded by saying, "I will give you respect when you are worthy of respect!" This exchange made its way to my parents before school was out that day. How? My uncle

> I CAN TRY TO MAKE PEOPLE EARN MY RESPECT, OR I CAN GIVE IT AND HONOR THE PART OF GOD THAT IS IN THEM.

Please be a good example

happened to be the Superintendent of the school. So, the first thing that happened when I got home was a meeting with my dad.

"We don't honor people because they are honorable, we honor them because we are honorable" was the first thing I remember him saying. He said, *"regardless of who this teacher is, or how they act towards you, you have a responsibility to honor and respect her because the way you respect others is a reflection of your respect and honor for yourself."*

There's so much depth to the topic of respect. But my dad showed me then, and continues to show me that respect is a gift that I give. I can try to make people earn my respect, or I can give it and honor the part of God that is in them. Ultimately, that's not up to them, that's up to me. If you make people earn your respect, you will be forced to earn your kids' respect too. If you show your kids that respect is a gift you give, they will give you the same gift.

KEELA

Respect was a big topic in our home growing up, and certain non-negotiables within our family were based on respect. Some families get it wrong because they equate respect with fear, which is not the same thing. Not everyone deserves your respect, but you, as parents, must model for your children how respect works. If you don't respect your wife or husband or your child, for that matter, how will they learn to respect you or others? I see it depicted often in movies. There is an abusive household where the dad or mom hits the kid in the face, and they say, "You need to respect me." But how do you expect your child to learn respect from showing them disrespect? It's antithetical to what you are trying to accomplish. The idea that your child needs to fear you does not mean they will respect you.

It is a choice to give respect to people, and not everyone deserves your respect. However, we can learn what respect means to God by reading Psalm 111:10: "The fear of the Lord is the beginning of wisdom; all those who practice it have a good understanding. His praise endures forever." Often, people do not have a healthy relationship with God and do not understand how to respect Him, so they can never contextualize what healthy respect looks like. While parents may love their kids, they can misunderstand the biblical approach to respect when they read the phrase *"fear of the Lord."* They act out the only way they understand respect can happen: through fear. However, this context in Psalms does not refer to being afraid of God in a terror-inducing sense. It signifies a reverential awe, respect, and deep reverence for God's authority. It is an attitude of humility and submission before God, recognizing His greatness, wisdom, and sovereignty. Fearing God is considered the starting point or foundation of wisdom. It acknowledges that God is the source of all true wisdom and understanding. When you approach God with reverence and a heart willing to submit to His will, it opens the door to gaining insight, discernment, and a deeper understanding of His ways. In the biblical context, *fearing the Lord* involves living according to His ways; fearing Him expresses love, trust, and devotion, leading to a desire to honor Him in all aspects of life.

When you understand the context of how we are to approach God, it helps us teach respect to our kids. We want our kids to love, respect, and trust us as parents, not just be afraid of us and comply. My dad always told my siblings and me that *intimacy is the breeding ground for respect, and respect is the breeding ground for love.* Intimacy is not easy; it takes work and doesn't happen by default. As you lead the way in your family, they will see fruit in your life and choose to respect that about you. When

Please be a good example

someone decides to respect you, you are likely going to become endeared to them. You can choose to love someone, but endearment takes respect and intimacy to another level in your family. I respected my parents as an authority, but it grew as I saw their fruit. What they lived and how they thought worked, and I wanted to see it work in my life, too.

WHITNEY

One day I was riding with my Dad in the car and he got pulled over by a police officer. The officer told him he was speeding. He said, "Yes Sir, I just wanted to tell you thank you for correcting me and helping me be better." The police officer didn't know what to say as he walked away with my dad's license trying to process what just happened. I was surprised at the police officer's response because anytime we got corrected, my parents always had us say, *"Thank you for correcting me and helping me be better."* I really didn't know that everyone didn't say things like that because it was so a part of what we did. I could tell the officer was uncomfortable. I asked my Dad why the officer walked away weirdly. He said that oftentimes people are disrespectful to the police and upset when they get pulled over so he was probably surprised. When the officer came back he apologized for his response but he was shocked at my Dad's response to being pulled over. He thanked him for his attitude and let him off with a warning.

Seeing my Dad say it and be so respectful showed me that I'll never

> ...WHEN YOU CHOOSE TO BE RESPECTFUL AND HAVE A GOOD ATTITUDE, THEN YOU ARE MORE LIKELY TO BE BLESSED AND BE GIVEN MERCY.

be too big or too old to humble myself, say those words, and show respect.

Recently, I got pulled over and my daughter Layla was with me. I got to have the same experience as my Dad in front of my daughter and was only given a warning. I knew it was due to my respect and my attitude because I deserved the ticket. This turned into a lesson on respect and attitude for Layla. I told her when you choose to be respectful and have a good attitude, then you are more likely to be blessed and be given mercy.

Also, in my house growing up and now in our house, we always say, "Yes sir" and "Yes ma'am." Those words and what we say when corrected show respect; it humbles us, and it sets our heart right. You can model it as a parent and you can also do the hard work of getting your kids to say these things. It's so much more than a saying... it's a shifting in their heart and in their mind. They are not going to like saying it but you are both going to like the outcome of a respectful nature in their lives.

TEACH ME HOW TO ACT

Dear Parent:

I don't know how to act! The way you respond in any given situation, will be my example of how I am supposed to respond. If you are gentle with me, I will learn to be gentle. If you are harsh with me, I will learn to be harsh. If you talk quietly with me, I will learn to speak quietly. If you yell and scream at me, I will learn to yell and scream at you and others.

Please be a good example

If you are easily offended by people, I will learn to be easily offended.

I will learn to respond, if you respond. I will learn to react, if you react.

I will learn to be positive, if you are positive. I will learn to be negative, if you are negative.

I will imitate your behavior. I will impersonate your character.

I will adopt your worldview as mine. You are the greatest influence in my life. It will be very hard for others to influence me the wrong way, if you will influence me in the right way.

Remember, I need an example who will lead me in the right way.

*Show me how to **act**, when people hurt you.*
*Show me how to **"Go On"** when people say you are through.*

*Show me how to **forgive**, when people do you wrong.*
*Show me how to **survive** and not lose my song.*

*Show me how to **give**; I need to be blessed.*
*Show me how to **live**, and not settle for second best.*

*Show me how to **see** the bright side of Life.*
*Show me how to **be happy**, in this world of strife.*

*Show me how to **Love**, when other people hate.*
*Show me the **power of words**, and my ability to create.*

*Show me how to **touch**, by reaching out to me.*
*Show me how to **Be**, all God has created me to be.*

*Show me how to **laugh**, and comfort me when I cry.*
*Show me how to **believe**, with my heart and not my eye.*

*Show me **all you can**; I need all the help I can get.*
*Show me **by your example**, what you sow, I will beget.*

Your Child.

JOSH

Everything in life is a result of how you think, your attitude and what you decide to do. Those are the only things that will determine what you have. **Think + Be + Do = Have.**

From the time I was very small, my dad would say things like:

> *"There's two kinds of people in the world; those who handle their frustration and those who wish they had."*
>
> *"You have to act your way into a feeling, not feel your way into an action."*
>
> *"You can't control what happens to you; you can only control your response to it."*
>
> *"You can live a life by design, or by default."*

Think, Be, Do. The way we think about life, people, and our circumstances will determine our attitude (Be). Our attitude will ultimately determine our actions. Too many people don't live their life intentionally. They don't intentionally consider how they think. They don't intentionally consider their attitudes. Most people

Please be a good example

tend to be led by their feelings, even people that claim to "have no feelings." It's always been interesting to me that the people that have no emotions really tend to have just one — anger. And it tends to be really strong. Whether you believe you can control your emotions or not is irrelevant.

Ultimately, whether you think you have emotions or not doesn't matter either. Why? Because your attitude is always your choice. Your attitude is what the Bible calls your "countenance." It is all the nonverbal cues you send, and ultimately how you decide to respond to what you think and how you feel. Sadly, because most people do such a poor job of controlling their thoughts and attitudes, they aren't intentional about what they do in life, or how they act.

These things are simple to understand, but not easy to live out. How do I know these things? Through the thousands of conversations I've had with my parents over the past 36 years. They are engraved into my heart like a sculptor engraves marble. **Think + Be + Do = Have.** I've seen my parents do this in many different ways. It has created an expectation that I now have of myself to intentionally practice equanimity and understand that at all times I am in control of my own thoughts, attitudes, and actions.

KEELA

One of the greatest lessons my parents taught me was that you shouldn't lead with a theoretical style of leadership, which, unfortunately, is the majority of what we see in the world. People have great thoughts and good things to say but do not consistently live a life of greatness. I have learned that the secret to my mom and dad's success is simple: they just kept doing what they knew to do repeatedly, even when they didn't seem to be getting the desired results. It was my parent's consistency that released the greatness others see today. Most people don't have a guidepost to follow because they don't see the Bible as relevant to their daily life or parenting. But the Bible is our guide and shows us how to live and act in all aspects of life. When you don't know what to do, you can find the answer within the truths in the Word of God. My mom and dad were constantly pointing us to the Word of God. They shared practical solutions for our everyday lives, inspiring me to discover God's wisdom personally.

> THEY JUST KEPT DOING WHAT THEY KNEW TO DO REPEATEDLY, EVEN WHEN THEY DIDN'T SEEM TO BE GETTING THE DESIRED RESULTS.

Being a theoretical leader is easy and takes no effort in the long term. What I saw in my home was transformational leadership. These are leaders who do not just talk; they take action. A Transformational leader lives out greatness daily and does what is best, even when no one is watching. I grew up in church and could see how many people "talked it" but didn't "live it." My parents wanted us to know how to act, and the best way to do that is to show your kids how to behave by modeling the actions you would like them to take. Your kids see how you and your spouse interact, and they see your responses to life. They know when you are frustrated, sad, or upset. Instead of acting like they don't see these things, I encourage you first to lead yourself so that you can also lead them to handle difficult circumstances. When I say lead yourself, I'm not insinuating that you always act like everything is okay. What helped me most was that my parents worked through what they needed to, but they also talked to me along the way so that I knew how to work through hard things.

Please be a good example

I remember one time in high school when my dad got very intense with me. I had been going through a lot in that season, but because of the intimacy we had built throughout my life, I decided to tell my dad that how he talked to me was not working. I explained that I couldn't hear what he was trying to say to me because of the intensity with which he was communicating it. I have a very strong personality, and sometimes, when you are wired this way, people talk to you strongly by default. I cannot assume to know all that he had personally dealt with that day that may have contributed to his intensity and I am sure what I did was frustrating. I could tell when I said that his approach hurt me it shocked him, but he led himself and asked me for forgiveness. He explained that while he needed to correct and lead me, he didn't want to hurt me. We cannot always do this for our kids at every moment, and sometimes we miss the mark, but I will always appreciate that my dad was open to hearing where I was in that season. This led to a greater understanding of our general interactions together. The main takeaway is that my dad was open to feedback, which inspired me to be open to feedback. Parenting is not a one-way conversation. Sometimes, you should listen to your kids if you want to have intimacy with them. This moment taught me how to be open to leading myself and show my kids how to treat others by treating them like that first. Often, we treat strangers better than those closest to us, which shouldn't be the case.

WHITNEY

Growing up and seeing the marriage, the friendships, the finances, the family, the relationships, the church, and legacy my parents have, makes me want to think, be, and do the way they do. If what they have is what I can have, then why wouldn't I follow in their footsteps?

My Dad taught us that you can live by default or by design. You can just respond to the world around you, or you can predetermine your response no matter what happens to you. Your kids will follow you in health or in un-health. If they look at what you have and it's not healthy, why would they follow you? Consider this: are you spiritually, relationally, physically, and emotionally someone worth following? Would you follow you and act like you?

I didn't see my parents asking me to act in ways that they weren't modeling. Every night with my kids, we go over our core values and the fruits of the spirit, which are love, joy, peace, patience, kindness, goodness, faithfulness, gentleness, and self-control. Layla, my oldest, was telling me the other day that self-control is the hardest one to do and I agree.

> YOU CAN JUST RESPOND TO THE WORLD AROUND YOU OR YOU CAN PREDETERMINE YOUR RESPONSE NO MATTER WHAT HAPPENS TO YOU.

Self-control is *the ability to control oneself, particularly one's emotions and desires, or the expression of them in one's behavior, especially in difficult situations.* More than anything else, your ability to exercise self-control and choose how you are going to act instead of just responding to life by default will teach your kids how they should act.

Please be a good example

3

Please don't penalize me for being a child

I need room to grow!

Dear Parent:

I am a child. I think like a child. Therefore, I reason like a child. I talk like a child. Therefore, I sound like a child. I walk like a child. Therefore, I stumble like a child. I eat like a child, Therefore, I am messy like a child.

What I am trying to say is that my ways are childish. I know this even though I do not understand it. I am different from you, but not much different, and certainly not for long.

When other people look at me, who do they think I look like? When you look at me, who do you think I look like? Well, they are right and you are right.

There is some of me that certainly does look like you. And you know what? Eventually, we will become more and more alike whether either of us like it or not.

At this time, we are alike, but we are also very different.

You are an adult and I am a child. This means from time to time, we think differently, we act differently, we talk differently, we express differently. Right now, I really want to be like you, but it is very difficult for me, because I am trying to find myself. By the way, do you really want me to be exactly like you?

I am a child, and I need room to grow. I need you to help me discover who I am.

Your Child

I Am a Child

I am a child, I need room to grow,
I am not an adult, there are many things I do not know.
I am a child, I am watching you,
Everything you say, and everything that you do.

You used to be a child, just like me,
How would you be different,
if through my eyes you could see?
I am a child, try not to forget.
"A young human being" in my ways not yet set.

JOSH

I once heard Denis Waitley say; *"You chose to have children, they didn't choose to have you."* That's a powerful thought. Most of us go through life with unsaid, and unmet expectations from people. Including our children. I think it is important to remember that you, as a parent, must show unconditional love to your children, but not expect unconditional love from them. After all, they're children. They are less wise, less mature and less capable of self-leadership than you.

The choice we make to have children places a requirement on us. Not on them. Whether that is how we talk to them, the content we expose them to, the conversations we have with them, or the people we put them around. We bear the weight of being the adult in the relationship.

Unfortunately, most of us go through more education to ride on an airplane for two hours than we do to have children. The government actually requires that we hear certain things every time we get on a plane. It doesn't matter if you're a million mile flier, you're going to hear the same briefing every time you get on a plane. I grew up flying all over the world with my parents. I think their safety briefing gives us a great template as parents of how to be on the journey of parenting.

1) **Fasten seatbelts securely:** In parenting, this means providing a stable and secure environment for children to grow and explore. Setting the right kind of boundaries for your children requires you to set the right boundaries for yourself as a parent. If you do not have your seatbelt on in life, neither will your children. Parents should model healthy boundaries and guidelines that help their children

Please don't penalize me for being a child

feel safe, while still allowing them the freedom to learn and develop.

My parents did this for me by having core values and living them out. Any expectation they created for me, they sought to live themselves. They didn't curse because they didn't want me to curse. They didn't spend time with the wrong people because they didn't want me to spend time with the wrong people. They managed their money, time, emotions, mental and spiritual health well and showed me how to do the same thing.

2) **Know your exits:** Airplane passengers are always shown the location of emergency exits. Similarly, good parents should be aware of potential risks and have a plan in place to address them. By teaching children about potential dangers and providing them with strategies to deal with difficult situations, parents empower their children to navigate the world confidently, while still being able to enjoy their childhood.

This isn't about being afraid, but you must be reminded that your children are children. They do not have a fully developed pre-frontal cortex. That means the part of their brain that enables them to think logically and have a healthy relationship with risk is not fully developed. That's why you're their parent. Teaching your kids about danger and risk, and giving them tools to address it, is not the same as teaching them to be afraid.

When I was growing up, we had 5 acres and a creek by our house. One day my dad asked me "Son, what would you do if a stray dog attacked you in the creek?" I had never thought that was a possibility until he mentioned it. I said, "I don't know." My dad said "You reach up into its neck, grab as hard as you can and try to rip its throat out." You may think that's hilarious, or gruesome. And that might not even be the best strategy if someone is getting attacked by a dog, but my dad taught me that I have to understand that even in a situation where I may feel powerless, I have power. He taught me the same thing when it came to bullies. As I've said throughout this book, I'm an introvert. I'm really not a person that looks for a fight. But my dad was the dad who taught me how to handle myself with a bully. "Son," he would say. "You can go get a teacher, but teachers usually show up after everything is over. If someone picks on you, or your sisters, or attacks you, don't worry about getting into trouble. You never need to start a fight, but you always need to end them." If you're a teacher reading this, you may not like that. My teachers didn't either. But throughout school I developed a reputation as someone who didn't get bullied or allow those in relationship to me to be bullied. That's not me bragging. My dad empowered me from a young age to know how to deal with difficult situations and people.

3) **Put your oxygen mask on first:** In the event of an emergency, passengers are instructed to put on their oxygen masks before helping others. This is a reminder to parents that they must prioritize their own physical and emotional well-being in order to effectively care for their children. By demonstrating self-care and personal growth, parents serve as positive role models and can better support their children.

If you are not healthy in spirit, soul and body, your children will not be healthy either. Another reminder: you are the adult. You set the tone for them. If you do not care for yourself, you teach them not to care for themselves. If you sacrifice your health for them, or anyone else, they will do the same. My parents regularly took vacations and trips without us to prioritize their relationship. They did weekly date nights as well. It wasn't just about us as their kids, they also continued to work on themselves.

> **IF YOU ARE NOT HEALTHY IN SPIRIT, SOUL AND BODY, YOUR CHILDREN WILL NOT BE HEALTHY EITHER.**

How many parents do we know that their whole identity is in their children, and when their children leave home, they have no identity? Your leadership is hopefully preparing your children to leave your home, not stay in it forever. So prepare for your future. Practice a weekly date night with your spouse. Take a weekend away from your kids once a quarter. Take a vacation once a year with just your spouse and "put your mask on." My parents did that, and it helped them, and helped us. Now my wife and I do the same thing, following in their footsteps.

4) **Remain seated and attentive:** Passengers on an airplane must remain seated and attentive during critical phases of the flight. As parents, it is essential to be present and engaged in your child's life, offering guidance and support when needed. By actively participating in your child's activities and interests, you foster a nurturing environment that allows them to flourish while still enjoying the freedom of childhood.

Your interests may not be your children's interests. You may not like the shows they watch, the toys they play with, or the activities they enjoy. Unless there are moral, ethical or core value concerns, engage with what your children enjoy. It is not their responsibility to enjoy what you enjoy. It is your responsibility to enjoy what they enjoy. I have a friend who was a division 1 baseball player because his dad wanted him to play baseball. He was never really interested in baseball, but his dad loved baseball, so there was an expectation for him to love baseball like his dad did.

My dad was an all-time great athlete. He tried out for the Dallas Cowboys and made the team. He was a local legend in Slidell, Louisiana where he went to high school. He went to college on a full ride scholarship as a basketball player. When I was in middle school, we would go play basketball together and he would run it like a practice. "Okay, son, I want you to do ten layups with your right hand, ten layups with your left hand, and then shoot ten free throws. We'll do that three times and then we'll do some dribbling drills." I just wanted to play HORSE, or shoot around. My dad knew that he could make me into a great basketball player, but he also realized in that season of my life that I didn't want to be a great basketball player. There was one particular time we went to the gym and I told him I didn't want to practice like that anymore. I said that if this was going to continue, I didn't want to go play with him anymore. From that time on, when we went to play basketball, we just played. No coaching. Looking back, it really would have helped me to have him coach me, but I wasn't interested. He did dunk on me quite a few times though. When I quit basketball in high school, my coach told me I was a "waste of potential" and that's probably true. But my dad would have ruined me if he coached me hard in that season of my life. I was more interested in video games. So he tried to take an interest in that with me as much as he could. He would play with me, or sit and watch and just talk to me. When I became the Student

Council president in high school, I started to ask him a lot about leadership. He mentored and coached me in how to be a leader then, and he still does now.

5) **Follow crew instructions:** Finally, passengers are advised to follow the instructions of the flight crew. This emphasizes the importance of parents being clear and consistent leaders in their children's lives. By setting expectations and consequences, parents can create an atmosphere of trust and respect that allows children to feel secure and confident in their exploration of the world.

Just like the crew on a plane, you're the leader. Your children are children. Not friends. In our home growing up, I was never confused about that. I didn't tell my parents when I was going to bed. I didn't tell them when I was going to school, or decide the kind of food I ate. They were flying the plane and I was a passenger. Your children do not know what is best for them. If your children are minors, God put you in their life to decide what is best for them. Just like God is in your life to decide what is best for you. God is the pilot of the plane of our lives, and parents are the crew. By being submitted to God and Godly authority in your life, you show your children how to submit to your authority. My dad has always said this, *"If you're too big to follow, you're too small to lead."* Too many parents can't lead their children well, because they are un-coachable, un-teachable, and dishonoring. If you follow a great leader, you can be a great leader. Model great

> TOO MANY PARENTS CAN'T LEAD THEIR CHILDREN WELL, BECAUSE THEY ARE UN-COACHABLE, UN-TEACHABLE, AND DISHONORING.

follower-ship for your children and you will show them how to follow you well.

KEELA

It can be almost natural to expect your kids to "get it." We forget that they are experiencing something new daily, learning and figuring out the world. Growing up, our parents taught us independence while still having clear expectations for us in various areas. Even now that I am a mom, I forget that the world around my kids is all so new, and they don't have context like I do. They may whine, cry, or ask a million questions, which can drive me crazy, but they need me to introduce them to the world around them. If they are only met with frustration or I brush them off, that is how they will deal with things in their world. Kids need to know they can do hard things and accomplish whatever they set their minds to as long as they are willing to pay the price. We need to provide a safe place for them to learn about the world and to be able to ask questions, or they will find another source to learn from. I want my kids to hear context about their world from me; my parents wanted the same with us. I never felt like I couldn't ask my parents questions.

There is a right time and place for questions. This is another thing you will have to teach your kids. However, they will learn most by what you do, not what you say. My parents modeled how they would want me to respond and act. This helped me so much because I could always reflect on their actions and model them with my siblings, friends, and others. I remember instances when my younger sister, Whitney, would ask me so many questions about everything, things as simple as why the sky was blue to what was happening in a movie I had never seen. I remember going to my parents, frustrated about having to answer all these questions,

Please don't penalize me for being a child

and I remember my dad asking me, *"Do I ever make you feel like I am frustrated when you ask me questions?"* Of course, my answer was no, and he explained that while he doesn't always feel like being asked a lot of questions, he is happy to take the time to answer my questions when he can because he loves me. He gave me the perspective that I should feel honored that she would seek me for answers because it shows how she sees me in her life. I always want my kids to feel like they can come to me about anything. Your kids should see you as an authority and a safe place to learn and grow. This will only change if you give them a reason to feel like they cannot freely come to you. I never felt that there was any topic I couldn't ask about or discuss.

> YOUR LIFE AND LESSONS ARE USEFUL FOR YOUR KIDS, AND BY SHARING WITH THEM, YOU CAN ENABLE THEM TO AVOID YOUR MISTAKES.

Our family was a safe place to learn, fail, and win. I want to create this same atmosphere in my home because it built so much confidence in my life. I felt like I had people on my side. I felt like I could bring things to my mom or dad because no matter how ridiculous or even frustrating it was at times, they were helping me shape my world and the way I saw myself. Through their actions and words, they empowered me with a godly perspective. If you do not speak to your kids and share the right way to do life with them, they will learn it from someone else. Your kids need your perspective. They need to know what you have learned and are still learning. Just because you are older doesn't mean you know everything. I remember my parents teaching me through their life lessons. Your life and lessons are useful for your kids, and by sharing with them, you can enable them to avoid your mistakes. My parents were approachable; they were open and honest with me. It taught me that I could also be open and did not need to hide things from those I loved and trusted the most. I learned I could use my imperfections for God and to help others. You are the greatest resource your child could ever learn from. Be a safe place for them and teach them through your life and your wins and losses how to be their best for God.

WHITNEY

When I think about my mom, I think of a lot of wonderful things and one of those things is "gentle patience." EPHESIANS 4:2 NLT says "ALWAYS BE HUMBLE AND GENTLE. BE PATIENT WITH EACH OTHER, MAKING ALLOWANCE FOR EACH OTHER'S FAULTS BECAUSE OF YOUR LOVE." This is my mom. She got her degree in elementary education and special needs. She has a heart for children and she also has the patience for them because she understands that they are developing. If there is anyone I want to be like holistically, it is my Mom. Knowing how she loved me, led me, encouraged me, and helped me grow makes me want to do the same for my kids. I often hear her voice in my head and when she is with me and my kids I allow her to correct me when I need it.

One day I was sitting at the dinner table and Layla was saying, "Mommy... Mommy!!... MOMMY!!!!!". I was in the middle of talking, and in front of everyone, I corrected Layla pretty intensely, because we have taught them how to interrupt us when we are talking. They are supposed to come and put their hand on us and wait until we stop the conversation to see what they need (My mom taught me that). After I corrected Layla, my mom whispered in my ear, "She doesn't need you to speak that intensely to her and you just really embarrassed her. You want your kids to always be able to come to you and you want to be interruptible. You didn't have to snap at her like that." My heart sank because

Please don't penalize me for being a child

she was right. I could have patiently and gently stopped and said, "Layla you know how to interrupt Mommy," but instead I was too intense. So now I need to apologize because she is growing. She is learning and so am I. I don't have it all figured out and I messed up. It is important for my kids to see me apologize when I am wrong just like my parents did with me.

My dad says to be a great lover you have to be a great apologizer and a great forgiver. In this case, I needed to remind her how to interrupt but I also now needed to apologize for how I came across. So I called her over and in front of my Mom apologized and told her I should not have spoken to her that way. I asked if I embarrassed her and she said I did. So I apologized for that too. I asked her what she needed and told her how much I loved her. Then I reminded her to interrupt the way we do in our house. After she went to sit back down, I asked my mom if there is anything I could do better because I am still growing and I need feedback. If I can't take it from my mom who is a great Mom then how can I give it to my girls and expect them to take it? We are all growing and getting better and we are similar in that, but I have the maturity to make room for their immaturity. I have to create a safe space for their growth... just like my Mom did and still does.

> TO BE A GREAT LOVER YOU HAVE TO BE A GREAT APOLOGIZER AND A GREAT FORGIVER.

LIFE IS A STRUGGLE

Dear Parent:

In my short life I am discovering that life is a struggle. There are many frustrations that I have, that may seem insignificant to you.

Do you remember how tough it is to crawl everywhere you go? I do. Can you remember how tough your first step was on your own two legs? Can you remember how hard it was for you to learn to get from your plate to your mouth? Talk about frustration! It's one thing to use your hand. I mean you can just grab a whole handful and try to shove it in your mouth, without getting too much on your face. But what about that thing called a fork! First of all, the food does not stay on it. Secondly, it hurts when you miss your mouth and hit your face.

Do you know how hard it is to figure out what article of clothing goes on what part of the body? I get so frustrated sometimes, when both of my legs go down the same leg of my pants and I get stuck. And what about shoes? How are you ever supposed to figure out what shoe goes on what foot? And shoe laces. Do they put shoelaces on shoes just to confuse young human beings like me?

Life is a struggle and I get frustrated enough without feeling like you get frustrated at me because I get frustrated about life. I get so confused sometimes and I feel like my confusion causes you to be confused. Please don't penalize me for being a child. I have a lot to learn. I need to be allowed to express my frustration, without you reminding me of how much of a baby I am.

Your Child

LIFE IS A STRUGGLE

Life is a struggle, it's the little things,
That gets people upset, and causes their bell to ring.
Just like a child, many adults whine and cry,
Rather than let the little things, go right on by.

Life is a struggle, I need room to grow.
I'm just a child, don't tell me I'm slow.
I'll grow up and be my very best,
If you will help me pass, life's little tests.

JOSH

In 2019, my dad wrote a poem called, **"Choose Your Hard"**

Being your best is hard
Being your normal is hard

Getting out of your comfort zone is hard
Staying in your comfort zone is hard

Making wise decisions is hard
Making bad decisions is hard

Starting a business is hard
Working for someone else is hard

Being in shape is hard
Being out of shape is hard

Making a lot of money is hard
Making a little bit of money is hard

Losing weight is hard
Being fat is hard

Being rich is hard
Being poor is hard

Working out is hard
Being weak is hard

Having great relationships is hard
Having bad relationships is hard

Being disciplined is hard
Being lazy is hard

Having friends is hard
Having no friends is hard

Fighting for your marriage is hard
Divorce is hard

Having a lot of things is hard
Having nothing is hard

Living on purpose is hard
Living off purpose is hard

Doing life God's way is hard
Doing life your own way is hard

Everything is hard! Choose your hard!

Life is full of challenges. As a child, my dad exposed me to great thinkers like Jim Rohn. One of his famous sayings is: *"Don't wish it was easier, wish you were better. Don't wish for less problems, wish for more skills. Don't wish for less challenge, wish for more wisdom.[1]"*

My parents taught me that there are two ways to do things in life: "the hard way and the most difficult way." Too many adults realize too late that all of life is full of hard things. This fact is unavoidable. We should teach our children that hard things aren't bad things. Think about the things that are hard for your children. Is putting a shirt on really that difficult? What about tying shoes? Going to the bathroom on a toilet? Walking? None of these things are hard for adults, but they are exceedingly difficult for children. Now think about your own life. What was really hard for you 5-10 years ago? Is it still as hard for you today as it was back then? I hope not. Otherwise, you haven't grown very much.

When I was 16, I learned how to drive a stick shift in my dad's Z06 Corvette. Talk about doing something the hard way. Not only was I trying to learn how to do something that seemed really hard, I was learning in a car that isn't built for learners. At 36, driving a manual transmission is no problem. But the first time I sat at a red light on a hill in that Z06 with cars behind me, I was sweating.

Please don't penalize me for being a child

Scared to death to roll back into the car behind me. I didn't like it, but I needed that experience in order to develop the comfortability I have today.

Why do kids need to learn how to embrace difficulty and struggle? Because, to do something you've never done, you've got to become a person you've never been.

That's the hard thing about hard things. It requires more out of me as a person that I currently am. But if I rise to the challenge today, I gain the power to become greater tomorrow. Think about how you see your kids. Why do you want them to tie their shoes, put on their clothes, bathe themselves, and brush their teeth on their own? Because one day they will have families of their own. And the struggles that the 5 year-old them experience pales in comparison to the struggles they will face as adults. It is an unavoidable truth of life. You see a version of them that they have no idea will exist. That version of them doesn't exist yet, but it will if they learn to do hard things well.

That's how God sees you too. God takes all the hard things in our life and uses them for good (ROMANS 8:28). If that's true, could there be a version of us that doesn't exist yet, that only God sees? Absolutely. You see yourself as you are today. God sees you at your highest potential. Every challenge in your life right now is meant to help you become the person you've never been so that you can do the things that you've never dreamed of doing. Be the kind of parent that buys into choosing your hard. You will raise unstoppable children if you do.

KEELA

Growing up, I often felt different and isolated. So much of growing up and maturing is facing hard things and, hopefully, learning how to overcome difficulties by allowing God to use them for your good. We will all face challenges in life, and the resistance and struggle enable us to grow. Some parents try to help their kids avoid battles, which will weaken them in the long run. As parents, we must stop rescuing our children from every hard thing and let them struggle with real-life issues, which is how they will grow. Our children develop courage, discipline, and character by facing adversity and challenges. Your kids need to know that the power of God enables us to be strong and have wisdom; it gives us the capacity to do whatever we set our minds to. One of the most powerful things my parents did was speak into my life and future daily. They did not do everything for me but supported me as I grew and dealt with what felt overwhelming as a kid. Your world is small when you are young, and minor issues can feel significant to you when you are a child, but there is power in perspective. As a parent, you can provide perspective to your child in an empowering way that speaks to who God made your son or daughter to be.

There was a time in high school when I struggled to see myself for who God made me to be. It was a challenge to be accepted because I was wired so differently than the other girls around me. I come across as very strong, and most people misunderstand me. I remember a specific night my dad came into my room and sat beside me. He knew I had been struggling with a few things, so he asked me, *"What is your name?"* I looked at him and smiled, but I was frustrated. I said, *"You know my name; you named me."* He told me that my name was Keela and that meant that I was the key. My dad explained how I could be the key to any situation in

Please don't penalize me for being a child

my life, meaning I didn't have to wait for other people to understand or accept me. I was the leader in every situation I walked into and could always bring solutions to any problem. I often remind myself of this, even today: just because I have grown older doesn't mean that I don't still struggle with similar issues.

> THE POWER IN YOUR LIFE IS IN WHAT YOU CAN CONTROL, NOT WHAT YOU CAN'T.

If you have ever felt different, you don't stop being unique because you get older. It is important how you approach your differences because the distinctive parts of you can change things for the better. So many people hyper-focus on feeling different, and they fail to recognize that God made them unique for a reason. I want to challenge you to focus on God's purpose and calling for your life over what others think or see. Stop focusing so much on your uniqueness or feeling isolated that you miss out on how God wants to use it. I now understand that God has a special purpose within my uniqueness. I know I don't have to be like everyone else. Leaders are never like everyone else anyway. That is what sets them apart. They think differently and do life differently. My dad has always told me, **"You cannot control what happens in life or what others do, but you can choose your response to it."** The power in your life is in what you can control, not what you can't. People waste time trying to control the uncontrollable, but when you know who you are in God, you aren't focused on uncontrollable things.

WHITNEY

My parents often admitted that they were not perfect. When I said things were hard for me, they didn't make me feel like that was stupid and I just needed to get over it. They always took time to understand why I felt that way and helped me change my mindset.

Growing up I struggled with my weight and I got made fun of because of it. My parents never blamed those who called me names, but they helped me see what was in my power to do. They would ask me questions like, "Did you give that person permission to hurt your feelings?" or, "We know this is hard and I'm sorry they said that, but remember, hurt people hurt people. How can you have compassion on this person saying unkind things?" I am sure they wanted to go fix it for me but they thought about the bigger picture. They knew that one day I would take the tools I was learning then and apply them to my much harder adult struggles. They shared with me examples of things they were facing and showed me how they were applying in their own lives the advice they gave me.

When you are young everything feels hard. Then we grow up and we think, "WHY DID I EVER THINK LIFE WAS HARD THEN?" However, we need to remember how we felt when we were young as we deal with our children now. We once felt like our kids feel and we need to let them know that. We can relate to their feelings. Sometimes parents hide their stories or their testimonies from their kids because they don't want them to repeat the same mistakes.

Sharing and talking about your struggle will make your kids less likely to repeat the same struggle or mistake. You hear a lot from teenagers that their parents "don't understand" but most parents actually do and are just unwilling to share the truth. Your kids already know you are not perfect and they need you to admit often that you are not. They need to hear that you wish you had applied in your life the advice that you are giving them now. They need to know your struggle and see that you came out better and

Please don't penalize me for being a child

> SHARING AND TALKING ABOUT YOUR STRUGGLE WILL MAKE YOUR KIDS LESS LIKELY TO REPEAT THE SAME STRUGGLE OR MISTAKE.

stronger. Everyone struggles. When they see that you struggled well, it will help them to do the same. I saw my parents struggle, but I saw them struggle like champions who knew they were going to win. Your kids need to know that it's okay to struggle but they can do it well.

DON'T MAKE ME FEEL SMALLER THAN I AM

Dear Parent:

Every time I look up at you, I am reminded how small I really am. I don't know if you can remember what it is like to have someone tower over you by several feet. I have a very strong neck because I am always looking up.

Size can be an intimidating thing, and sometimes it is. I am intimidated when you come walking fast towards me with a mean look on your face. I am intimidated when you feel like you have to raise your voice to me to get your point across, because you are angry or you do not think I am listening to you. These are just a few things that make me feel smaller than I really am.

But, I also want you to know that when I am with you and you are by my side, I feel as big as you, because I am with you.

One other thing you might want to be aware of: When I feel like your big friends are more important than me, because they are big like you, it makes me feel smaller than I really am.

REMEMBER:
You are big, I am small.
I am short, you are tall.
You are complex, you have been around.
I am simple, just getting off the ground.
Little things make me laugh and little things make me cry.
But you, you are much older, more mature than I.
The ability you have, is to make me feel big.
But beyond your emotions, you will have to dig.

When I get upset and tangled inside.
I need you to help me, and be my loving guide.
I'll never be as big as I might have been.
If you don't remind me, I was made to win.

When I come into a room, don't tell me to go play.
First, just touch me, and then send me on my way.
I want to be big, to be just like you.
So make me feel big, like only you can do.

Your Child

JOSH

When I was very little, I can remember many times when my dad would kneel down to talk with me face to face. He's 6'6" so it's a long way to go to come down to a toddler's level. I know this from experience now. I'm 6'5" and do the same thing with my kids. He wouldn't just do this when I was in trouble, he would

Please don't penalize me for being a child

do this when he wanted to connect with me intentionally. He would also pick all of us up and have us ride on his shoulders. That made us see the world how he saw it. He would also never let us walk past him without touching our heads or grabbing us, hugging, and kissing us. Getting on our level was a lot easier for my mom. She's 5'3" so we were close to the same height when I was at a relatively young age.

As I got into school, my mom would intentionally come into my spaces and connect with me. Many nights, after we got home from school, ate dinner and ended up in our rooms, my mom would come to my room and just sit in there with me. She would do this because she knew me. She didn't have to ask me questions or do some deep digging. She knew if she sat there long enough, I would just start talking, and everything I was processing would blast out like a fire-hose. That was her "getting on my level" and connecting with me in the way that best worked for me. Another method might have worked for her, but she intentionally figured out how to connect with me. If she would have asked me how to connect with her, I could not have given her an answer. My mom was intentional about making me feel big in her eyes by doing that.

My dad is a passionate man. He cares deeply, expresses loudly, and loves extravagantly. I don't remember him ever yelling at us, but he was frequently intense. Many intense men ruin their children with their intensity. Although my dad was and is an intense man, he did something intentionally to not make us feel small. He apologized A LOT. He said, "I'm sorry" to us as much as he said, "I love you." When you apologize to your children, you give them the power to forgive. You give them the opportunity to be the "bigger person." My dad never made me feel small, and it wasn't because he was a timid man who never raised his voice.

He made me feel big, because when he made a mistake, he owned it, apologized, and worked to get better. Parents who are passionate and care deeply are going to have to apologize frequently, because their passion can quickly translate into over-caring. The more passionate you are, the more you will have to apologize. That's what will prevent your children from feeling small as they grow up.

> **WHEN YOU APOLOGIZE TO YOUR CHILDREN, YOU GIVE THEM THE POWER TO FORGIVE. YOU GIVE THEM THE OPPORTUNITY TO BE THE "BIGGER PERSON."**

KEELA

I saw my parents as superheroes when I was little, which is typical for children. You think your parents have all the answers to life. As you become a teenager, this changes, and you come to the realization that your parents know nothing, and you know everything. As you continue into adulthood, you have this epiphany: you have so much to learn and know nothing. You start to reflect on your parents and understand they knew much more than you gave them credit for. As a parent, you carry so much weight with your children. This is why many people have mother and father issues into adulthood. These issues affect every part of a person's life and become the filter through which they see everything. I saw a quote recently that said, ***"Speak to your children as if they are the wisest, kindest, most beautiful, and most magical humans on the earth, for what they believe is what they become."*** [2] How you speak to and treat your children will shape how they view themselves and others for a lifetime. I remember my parents speaking positively over us; they would speak to the giftings they believed God had given us. They encouraged us to bring the best parts of ourselves into whatever room we walked in and challenged us when we did not live up to the greatness they knew was inside us.

> How you speak to and treat your children will shape how they view themselves and others for a lifetime.

Most importantly, they corrected and directed us with love. They never called us stupid or made us feel like an inconvenience. We knew we were important to them. In any season, I could call my dad, and he would answer, no matter who he was with. Our family was the priority, and we felt that. Frustration comes with everyday life, and often, your kids add to that unintentionally.

There are seasons when we can feel burned out, but the investment that you are making in your family will last beyond your lifetime. Your actions and interactions create neural pathways your child will carry forever, shaping brain functions. Neural pathways connect neurons, and they light up when you think or experience something for the first time. These connections form a pattern in your brain and now have an attached meaning. Research shows that certain experience-based brain and biological developments happen within the early years of our lives. These neuropathways can set trajectories that affect future competence, health, emotional regulation, and more. Now, we have a greater understanding of how a family environment affects brain development in our early life. So, while you may not always see the effects you have on the children God entrusted you with, their brains and even bodies respond in a way that will affect them for the rest of their lives. As I have gotten older, my parents' presence in my life and the effects they have had continue to shape me for the better.

While my viewpoint has matured, and I can see them as fallible humans, their daily choices and interactions with me constantly inspire me. They have always made the decision to be people who speak into me, no matter how old I am, and this has had irrevocable effects on my life.

WHITNEY

I remember the feeling of holding onto my Dad's leg. I remember the feeling of my tiny hand in his huge hand. It was as if my hand would disappear in his. Instead of making me feel small, my dad has a way of making me feel special, powerful, and seen. I was never interrupting him and never in his way. In fact, he wanted me in his way and in his space.

With both my parents there was never a conversation that was too small or unimportant to talk about. As a 32 year old woman, they still make me feel this way. I can call anytime or interrupt them and they will take time for me. I remember when my Dad was in a season of being in big meetings with current and former world leaders. I called him and he answered, "Hey Baby, I am sitting with President George Bush, but you know I will always take your call no matter who I am with. Do you need me right now or can I call you back?" I was stunned and knew he had told me he would always answer but this made me feel beyond special and valued. He has made a point to always put our family before anything else or anyone else. I felt as a child and still do as an adult... massively important in their lives.

Please don't penalize me for being a child

HELP ME TO GROW

Dear Parent:

There will be no time in my life that I will be so eager to grow as I am right now. I want to grow physically. I want to grow mentally and emotionally. I want to grow spiritually. My body, soul, and spirit are longing for growth.

I need you to be looking for ways to help me grow in these areas. I am hungry to experience anything and everything that you will put in front of me at this crucial time in my life. So please, choose well. If what you give me does not truly satisfy me in these three areas, I will have to search for a lifetime, trying to find fulfillment in all three of these areas.

I am a tri-dimensional being. In other words, my body is fed when I give it food. My mind is fed when I give it food. My spirit is fed when I give it food. If I starve one of these areas of my being, I am incomplete. I need you to help me grow.

You can help me grow by exposing me to proper nutrition, in all three areas. You first do this by availing yourself to personal growth. For as you grow, I will grow.

Let me give you some practical examples of what I am talking about. If you are a person that wants the best for yourself in life, I will know you want the best for me. If you are a person who understands that you get what you want in life by helping others get what they want, I know that you will be committed to helping me grow, so that growth can take place in your own life.

More specifically, if you read to me, it will cultivate my mind, and I will become a reader. If you feed me the right foods to eat, I will come to appreciate what is good for me, based on what you have given me. If you pray for me, I will learn to pray for you, and furthermore, value prayer as a necessary ingredient for my spiritual growth. If when you tell me stories, and I love stories, you will include true stories, like "THE GREATEST STORY EVER TOLD", about the gift of Salvation that God gave us through His Son, Jesus, I will grow spiritually and learn to think rightly.

> IF YOU ARE A PERSON THAT WANTS THE BEST FOR YOURSELF IN LIFE, I WILL KNOW YOU WANT THE BEST FOR ME.

Please don't penalize me for being a child, I need room to grow and I need your help to grow.

Your Child

JOSH

It will be hard for you to take your children to a place you've never been. If you are emotionally, financially, mentally, spiritually, or physically undeveloped, they will probably be too. How many children grow up with no concept of how to manage their personal finances because their parents didn't? How many people spend much of their adulthood learning about nutrition and physical discipline because their parents never understood or taught them?

From the time I was little, my dad had a library full of books. When he had downtime he was reading. When we were on vacation, he was reading. When we were in the car, he was listening to Zig Ziglar, Jim Rohn, Earl Nightingale, Tony Robbins, and other great thinkers. Even though my dad traveled most nights, when he was home, he would sit with all of us and read a bible story and devotion before we went to bed. When he wasn't there, my mom would do it. That developed a love of learning within me. I now practice the same habits that I saw my dad practicing.

Both of my parents are supremely disciplined physically. They exercise every day and rarely miss a workout, even in their 60's. Growing up, it could be frustrating for us, because it would often happen when we were on vacation. My dad would say, ***"You don't become undisciplined just because you change your location."*** There were days we would wake up and before we did anything fun, my parents would say, "We're going to the gym." That didn't happen all the time or on every vacation, but it still happens to this day. Often, when my dad and I travel together, the first thing we do is go find a gym.

Specifically regarding the Bible, my parents used the **Beginner's Bible** when we were children, and as we got older, we used the **Hurlbut's Story Bible**, which is one of the greatest chronological story Bibles that exists.

KEELA

Through my parents' example, I have learned that all of us will grow, but you get to decide if you will grow better. Have you ever looked at your yard and wondered why weeds can grow anywhere? They thrive through concrete cracks or in areas where nothing grows successfully. This is how we grow by default; everything within your default can grow without much effort. Your default is what comes naturally to you; it is the way you see, feel, or think about the world without trying. If you do not pay attention, your life will resemble the weeds that can overtake your garden or yard. Often, we don't even realize we are feeding the growth of unhealthy things in our lives because we cannot identify our defaults. The standard ways you think, feel, and operate are like a weed. Your defaults will get you somewhere, but most likely, you will end up in places, relationships, and situations you never really wanted because you are not living by design. People who specialize in landscape design approach things with an intentional mindset. First, they would need to remove the overgrowth that does not contribute to the overall environment. If we want to grow with intention, we must also remove the overgrowth of unhealthy things. You can do this by looking at what has been learned or applied from your parents or others and then deciding what you want to carry or pass down to those around you.

> **YOU ARE THE DESIGNER OF YOUR LIFE AND MUST HAVE A VISION FOR WHAT IT WILL LOOK LIKE.**

Incredibly, a landscape designer can envision something beautiful in the middle of what can look like a mess. You are the designer of your life and must have a vision for what it will look like. No matter how you grew up, ask yourself what your life could be like. Answering that is where you discover what is possible outside of defaults. My parents helped me develop a vision for my life. They would ask me questions like, *"What do you see for your life?"* and

"What are you passionate about?" They constantly encouraged me to see a future for myself and make decisions based on that. My dad is a visionary and always thinks about what is possible. I am thankful for my parents' guidance; many people look back at their lives and see what has happened but do not think about what is possible for their future. I was taught that living a life by design means you think about and take action on what is possible. My dad was always reading and studying; he has had libraries and books centered on the things of God and leadership our whole life. I remember I could walk into his library and tell him a topic I wanted to learn more about, and he could go right to a section out of hundreds of books and not only find the right book but talk to me about his takeaways from it. He taught me to write takeaways in the book I was reading and to date it so I could go back and see my growth and what I had learned in that season. In most of the books he let me read, I would find that he had read it multiple times, and each time, it had built onto his previous takeaways.

> A LEADER RECOGNIZES WHAT THEY CAN LEARN FROM OTHERS AND APPLIES THAT WISDOM.

People say readers are leaders, but my dad always said that leaders are readers. He taught me that anyone can read a book, but that doesn't necessarily make them leaders. A leader recognizes what they can learn from others and applies that wisdom. PROVERBS 4:7 says, "THE BEGINNING OF WISDOM IS THIS: GET WISDOM. THOUGH IT COST ALL YOU HAVE, GET UNDERSTANDING." Wise people know they need wisdom, and there are people who have life experiences and lessons you could not learn on your own. I saw both of my parents seek out and apply Godly wisdom. One of the most incredible things they did to help me grow was to grow themselves. We won't always have the answers for everything, but we can be people who look and seek answers. This helped to develop my desire to study the things of God personally. When I did not understand something, I would seek out the answer. This built my confidence and helped me know what faith looks like. Not everything has an answer, and that's okay, but it's also okay to ask and research. I was never scared of "not knowing" because my parents weren't "know-it-alls" with me and taught me that it's okay not to know. You can still choose to grow better, no matter what, when you grow by design and don't settle into living by your defaults.

WHITNEY

Growing up, we had a lot of family meetings and we never knew what they were going to be about beforehand, other than it was for spending time together and for our growth. They could just be reading *"The Book Of Virtues"* by William J. Bennett, or it could be about a certain topic they wanted to discuss. Either way it was and still is, as 30 year old adults, not always fun to have family meetings. We all have seen since we were young, the benefit of these meetings and the benefit of conflict. These meetings were not just conflict between each other but also the conflict of personal growth. Nothing is off limits in our family. Now, as adults that work and do ministry together, we often have conflicts that need to be resolved but this process makes us better altogether.

Family meetings were intentional, and still are, for my parents to pour into us, not just as their kids, but as their mentees that are the physical manifestation of their legacy. They care so much about our growth and us reaching our full God-given potential, that they have gone above and beyond to make sure they do

Please don't penalize me for being a child

everything in their power for that to happen. Naturally, I don't like conflict but growing up in a family that embraces it, helped me to see the benefit of it.

Not only by seeing the way my parents live, but by their initiating intentional family connection focused on our growth, I am challenged to be healthy in spirit, soul, and body.

4

Spend time with me

we don't have much time together.

TO EVERYTHING THERE IS A SEASON

Dear Parent:
One of the definitions for **Season** is, *"A specific time of year when something is common or plentiful or when an activity takes place."* So, Season can be defined as, "A specific time in life, in which, specific things take place."

The Bible says in the book of ECCLESIASTES, the third chapter,

> "TO EVERY THING THERE IS A SEASON, AND A TIME TO EVERY PURPOSE UNDER THE HEAVEN: A TIME TO BE BORN, AND A TIME TO DIE; A TIME TO PLANT AND A TIME TO PLUCK UP THAT WHICH IS PLANTED; A TIME TO KILL AND A TIME TO HEAL; A TIME TO BREAK DOWN, AND A TIME TO BUILD UP; A TIME TO

WEEP, AND A TIME TO LAUGH; A TIME TO MOURN, AND A TIME TO DANCE; A TIME TO CAST STONES, AND A TIME TO GATHER STONES TOGETHER; A TIME TO EMBRACE AND A TIME TO REFRAIN FROM EMBRACING; A TIME TO GET, AND A TIME TO LOSE; A TIME TO KEEP AND A TIME TO CAST AWAY; A TIME TO REND, AND A TIME TO SEW, A TIME TO KEEP SILENCE AND A TIME TO SPEAK; A TIME TO LOVE, AND A TIME TO HATE; A TIME OF WAR, AND A TIME OF PEACE.[3]"

There is a PURPOSE for every TIME and a TIME for every PURPOSE.

This Season in my life is very important. My ability to survive and grow during this Season, will determine my ability to flourish in the next Season. I need you to help me understand what my Purpose is during this crucial Time in my life. You can best do this, by choosing to spend time with me.

By spending time with me, I develop a sense of Purpose. When you choose to spend time with me, it helps me to understand my purpose for being. I really want you to understand that there is absolutely no one else I would rather spend time with than you. This desire I have to spend time with you is not something that had to be developed. I am automatically drawn to you. I really can't help it.

> WHEN YOU CHOOSE TO SPEND TIME WITH ME, IT HELPS ME TO UNDERSTAND MY PURPOSE FOR BEING.

There are several very important reasons why I need you to spend time with me:

1. I will learn the most important purpose for my existence. The most important purpose for my existence on this earth is to have RELATIONSHIP. It is only through successful interpersonal relationships that we find happiness on this earth. The fact is, we were created specifically to have a relationship with God. We must spend time with God, know God, and thus begin to understand ourselves and our purpose for existence. Without spending time with God, not only do we not know Him, but we never gain our own sense of purpose.

   I need you to spend time with me, because it will help me to have a sense of purpose in life through an understanding of the importance of relationships. I will never find my purpose through the things that you possess and accumulate for you or me. I will never understand my purpose through the material things that you give me.

   I NEED YOU TO SPEND TIME WITH ME. This is the Season in which I need to discover the most important purpose for my existence: to have RELATIONSHIP.

2. I will learn to seize opportunities that lie before me. An opportunity is defined as, "a time or set

of circumstances that are suitable for a particular purpose." The ability to seize opportunities comes as a result of understanding Time and Purpose.

I need you to spend time with me, so that I will recognize opportunity when it knocks. In other words, the opportunity you have to teach and the opportunity I have to learn will be maximized. I will learn bad from good, or good from bad, based on what you teach me, by spending time with me.

If in fact, God created me on purpose, for a purpose, I want to seize the opportunities He gives me. Just so you know, I believe the greatest opportunity I will ever have on this earth is the opportunity I have right now to be with you. There is no greater joy I have in life than to be with you.

3. I will learn the value of Time. Time is defined as, "an occasion or instance." Once time has passed, it can never be recovered.

TIME
Time is relevant, only when it is discovered,
Time that is lost cannot be recovered.
Each person is given, a specific amount of time,
To waste what has been given, is the worst kind of crime.

Time has been given, from God above,
Time to enjoy, and learn how to love.
Time is to be spent, with family indeed,
Time is the invisible, heavenly seed.

We have but a moment, the blink of an eye,
Let's spend time together, before we say good-bye,
Time and Purpose, they go hand in hand,
By spending time with you, I'll know where I stand.

Time can be wasted, or be well-spent;
Let's catch what we have, and we won't wonder where it went.
Spend time with me, you are my best friend.
If you do now, I'll be with you in the end.

Your Child

JOSH

A few years ago, I wrote a book called **The Way to Live**. In that book I reference the *Harvard Study of Adult Development* [4]. It is one of the longest studies ever done on adult life.

It began in 1938 with 268 Harvard sophomores, the study continues today with over 1,300 of these men's offspring as well as other families from around Boston. Overwhelmingly, this study provides evidence that the greatest predictor of a good life is the quality of a person's relationships.

The greatest thing you can do for your children is to have a great relationship with them. That will teach them to have great relationships with other people, but it will also ensure that they live a great life. And great relationships are only established through quality time.

Over the past 50 years, the amount of time parents spend with their children has been on the rise. According to recent statistics, married fathers spend an average of 6.5 hours a week with their children, and married mothers spend close to double that, 12.9 hours. That seems like it would lead to good outcomes. But more than half of parents with children under the age of 18 report feeling "distant" from their children.

There's a simple answer for this. Spending time with your kids is not the same as spending "quality" time with them. You may spend time with your kids, but how much of that is watching TV, being at a game, or sitting in the same room on phones and digital devices?

It's been said that we get 18 summers with our kids. That's not really true. We probably get less summers than that. By the time your child is 12, you will have already spent 75% of the time you get with them in your lifetime. Once our children hit middle school, they have their own social network, extra-curricular activities, and commitments. Once they start driving, we will see even less of them. That doesn't mean that you won't have any more time left, but think about it. 75% of all the time you get with your kids happens before they turn 12. It is so easy to take this time for granted. It's also easy to think that the best time we get with our kids is when we go on trips, or have events to attend. Again, that's time, but not quality time.

Here's some good news: that wasn't true for my family growing up, and it doesn't have to be true for yours either. Even now, I speak to my parents daily and I spend time with them weekly. Our family takes at least one trip yearly all together with my parents, our spouses, and our kids. My dad was my best man in my wedding and he really is my best friend. But, from the time I was born until I was 12, my dad was gone from Sunday to Thursday, 40+ weeks a year traveling, speaking, and preaching. If anyone was a dad that missed time with his kids, it would be my dad. But that didn't happen, because for him it wasn't about quantity, it was about quality. When he was with us, he was fully present. He wasn't taking sales calls, or meeting with people in an office somewhere. I'm sure that led to missed opportunities and sacrifices. But how many parents sacrifice time with their kids to complete one more project, call one more client, or close one more deal? My parents chose the opposite. One more moment with us was more important than one more opportunity, deal, or client.

> ONE MORE MOMENT WITH US WAS MORE IMPORTANT THAN ONE MORE OPPORTUNITY, DEAL, OR CLIENT.

When I was growing up, we didn't have to combat the intrusion of social media and cell phones, but there were still plenty of interruptions. My parents had a couple of intentional things they did with us that may help you to be deliberate about how you spend time with your kids.

Earlier in the book, I talked about how we did bedtime when we were really young. My parents would bathe us, read us a devotional or bible story, pray for/with us, and then we would go to bed. We also ate dinner together as a family every night that we could. We didn't do it every night, but at least 3 nights a week, we would all sit down at the dinner table together at the same time. My dad would have intentional questions he would ask us about our family core values, how our week was going and what

Spend time with me

we love about each other. What a lot of parents I know do - which is also a great strategy - is "highs, lows, buffalos." This is where you talk about the highs and lows of your day, and then the buffalo is something that happened that you didn't expect. In addition to having dinners together, one night a week, we had a family gathering. Usually this would take place before/after dinner and my parents would spend time with the three of us encouraging us, correcting us, and directing us. We would also talk about what we needed to do to help us get along better with each other. Sometimes those family gatherings were topical. Sometimes they were just to connect, but it was intentional time that we spent together.

My parents also took us with them wherever they went, as much as they could. When my dad would do crusades, we would drive with him and my mom in a conversion van all over America. We also took regular family vacations. Sometimes these were at different times than when school was out, and my parents dealt with conflict at our school because of that. Their priority was not making sure we were "in school" but making sure we were with them. They still prioritized our education, but they were busy entrepreneurs and were intentional about taking us away when their schedule allowed.

When we would go on family vacations, it was always just our family that went. I remember friends that would take their friends on vacations, and I had friends that would invite me on their vacations too. My parents never allowed us to do that, because they wanted our family to be together. If they were going to spend the money on a trip, they would spend it on a family trip for our family to be together. That level of intentionality was like night and day compared to most of my friends.

The summer I turned 15 and was getting ready to go into high school my dad told me I would never have a summer again where I didn't work. However, my job would be different from most summer jobs. My dad said my job for that summer was just to "be with him." All summer I would go where he went and do what he did. If he was in meetings, I was with him. If he was speaking at a conference, I was with him. If he was doing yard work, chores, errands or anything else, I was with him. He paid me all summer just to be with him. It wasn't about what we did, it was about being together.

My parents had a vision for us to be together. They wanted us to be a family that did what we did together, all through life, and that plan went into effect very early in our lives.

To this day, we all work together, and we work hard to make it work. In our 30's, we still have regular Craft family meetings—sometimes with our spouses and sometimes without them. We still talk to each other as siblings a lot and spend a lot of time with my parents because of the time that they intentionally spent with us.

KEELA

As a parent, you only have 18 years maximum to spend unlimited time with your child. If your child is 10, you have eight more summers with them until they are launched into adulthood. Life can seem so busy, and time can pass so fast that we miss moments. In our family, there were specific times when my parents would stop and tell us to take in the moment. Sometimes, as a family, we would take the time to share how we felt, what we learned, or what we were inspired by within a moment. One time, we were in Colorado, and my dad saw a plaque with a quote by Maya Angelou: **"Life is not measured by the number of breaths** *we take, but by the moments that take our breath away."* [5] My dad could have just walked by and thought, that's a great quote. Instead, he brought us all to the entrance of the house and had us all look at it. He described what he felt when he read it and cried; he then asked us what we thought when we read it. This is just an example of an everyday occurrence in our family. Because of my parents, we learned to seize moments daily and understand why they were important. There was always a lesson or something we could learn from. My parents did not allow themselves to be rushed. I never felt that way in my family. We would take the time we needed to do what was most important. Other things could wait because being together and learning together was the highest priority. It gave me a unique outlook on life to not allow outside things or pressure from others to set my priorities.

> THE MIRACLES IN LIFE ARE FOUND IN THE EVERYDAY MOMENTS.

Spending time together was one of the most essential things in my family. This helped me to value my time with my kids on a level that most families do not. I realize there are moments I will never get back if I miss them. People see everyday things happening and devalue those moments, but those moments are the exact ones you regret or miss later in life. Psalms 90:12 says, "Teach us to number our days, that we may gain a heart of wisdom." If we could understand that we only have this one life on earth and see what a moment means, we would put a different weight on the everyday occurrences we let pass by. In his book Your Divine Fingerprint, my dad says, "Your moments can create momentum that enables a miracle to happen." Miracles in life are found in the everyday moments. I am so grateful that my parents showed me how special being together was and that we took every moment as a family. The power of God has been released in my life because my parents showed me how God works in my everyday, seemingly ordinary moments and talked to me about it.

WHITNEY

If there was one thing my parents did, it was being intentional. No matter how we spent time together, there were intentional look-each-other-in-the-eye meaningful conversations, and biblical life lessons that would apply to us. Not only did this shape who I am, but it let me know that my parents love me and want to be with me. There is a deeper meaning in everything we do.

I remember this one time our family went to see a movie. I am pretty sure it was a cartoon that was mostly funny but when we got in the car my Dad asked us all to give a "takeaway" from the movie. I started laughing because I thought he was joking but he was serious. A takeaway is just answering the question— *"What was your personal lesson?"*— in any conversation, movie, or even song. Not only can you learn something from anything or anyone, but my parents taught us early that God can speak to you through anything and anyone.

> **IF THERE WAS ONE THING MY PARENTS DID, IT WAS BEING INTENTIONAL.**

After the movie we all took turns giving our takeaway in the car, and when it was Dad's turn, I was amazed at how profound his was. It inspired me to be intentional with how I see everything and to always be listening to what God may be wanting to say to me. People may think that seeing a movie isn't spending time with people you love, but that depends on what you make it. You have so much power to create intentional moments, no matter what you are doing, that will make your kids feel loved, seen, valued, and special.

IT'S THE LITTLE THINGS THAT MATTER MOST

Dear Parent:

I heard a song the other day. The name of the song is, "**Cat's in the Cradle,**[6]" by Harry Chapin. That song says what I feel. It's the little things that matter most to me. Being around me, playing with me, and being together is what is most important to me. If you do the little things with me now, I'll always want you around for big things in my life.

Your Child

JOSH

I grew up singing this song with my dad all over the United States. We would sing this song, and then afterward my dad would talk to parents in the audience about the parenting stats listed earlier in this book. He would encourage them not to be the parents in this song, but to be the parents God wanted them to be. When I think about this song, I think about how my parents built our relationship through little things.

Whether you realize it or not, your presence as a parent is the most important gift you can give to your child. Even the smallest moments of connection, like sharing a meal, reading a bedtime story, or playing a game together, can have a profound impact on your child's emotional well-being. Prioritize spending quality time with your children, regardless of how busy life may get.

My dad had a home office when I was growing up, and I would frequently interrupt him when he was on a call or working. He never said he was too busy for me, or made me feel like something else was more important than me. He would allow me to interrupt him and talk with him about whatever I wanted to talk with him about. He was an active listener to my thoughts and feelings and showed me he valued those things.

Now, more than ever, it is so easy for us as parents to sit on our phones and be half-engaged with our kids. Honestly, that's how we're doing most things now. We sit in meetings on our phones, drive while we're on our phones, we go on dates with our spouses and are on our phones. We go on vacation, and for many of us, our first priority is to pull out our phones to take a picture. We find ourselves progressively being unable to be fully present in a moment because we want the moment to be shared elsewhere. What many busy parents tend to do is try to make grand gestures while they don't do little things well.

> WE FIND OURSELVES PROGRESSIVELY BEING UNABLE TO BE FULLY PRESENT IN A MOMENT BECAUSE WE WANT THE MOMENT TO BE SHARED ELSEWHERE.

My parents didn't have a lot of money growing up, and as they made money, it would have been easy for them to just give us "stuff" as a token of their love, because they didn't get to have a lot of stuff. I have quite a few friends who grew up in poverty that buy their kids every conceivable thing they desire, because they didn't get that growing up. But that's not what your kids need. Your kids do need something you probably never got. But it's not a trip to Disney World, or another toy. Your kids need your full focus, attention, and love. Our lives should not be like Cat's in the Cradle. I don't want my kids to have to wait for me to "have

Spend time with me

a good time then." I want to do my best to make sure we have a good time now. Even if the moment isn't perfect, or it's an interruption in my life, that's better than trying to craft some kind of perfect moment in the future that may never come.

My parents spent the time, effort, and energy with me that they had "today." To my knowledge, they gave me everything that they had every moment they were with me, regardless of whether the timing or planning was perfect.

One particular time, my dad was flying home from a work trip and told me he would take me to the park when he got home. His plane experienced major delays and he didn't arrive home until 2AM in the morning. The first thing he did when he came home was wake me up in the middle of the night and take me to the park. Was that optimal for my schooling? Or his schedule? Not at all, but I still remember the memory. It's not about making sure "the good time" happens in the future. It's about making the good time happen right now in this moment.

I think the same way about my kids. I've already kept them up late playing with them when I've come home late. Because some days, spending time together is more important than the routine. I've awakened them late at night just to love on them, even though they are tired the next day. Because as I got older, the times my dad did that meant more to me than taking an expensive trip somewhere, or getting a new toy when he came home.

Just like this song, your kids are going to grow up to parent like you parent, and when they are adults, they are going to prioritize their relationship with you, the way you prioritized your relationship with them when they were children. I am fully confident that I love spending time with my parents now, because they loved spending time with me then. And I want to grow up to be just like them with my kids.

KEELA

There are unique things that have connected me to each of my mom and dad. I have always loved being close to my mom; her touch has been what I would describe as healing. And my dad's words and presence have always made such a significant impact on my life. As parents, we often discount the fact that the smallest and most consistent things we say or do build up and mean much more than we ever intended for the positive. However, our words and actions can negatively influence or impact our kids. Thankfully, I have always had more positive than negative input from my parents. There have been instances in life when I could draw from the well of my heart and mind all they have poured into me.

High school was tough for me. I was molested earlier in my life, around 11 or 12. It's hard to remember fully. I did not tell my parents what had happened until four years later.

I hadn't told them because I thought it was my fault. I couldn't understand why I would let that happen because I did not want it to happen. As I have mentioned before, I am strong and have no problem standing up to people or holding my ground. But I couldn't account for what happened or why I didn't fight back in this situation. I tend to isolate myself and try to figure things out independently, which isn't always healthy. Time went on, and small things affected me, like a residue I couldn't eliminate until I was honest with my mom and dad. I didn't know how to start the conversation because I wasn't sure how to explain it.

Spend time with me

As time passed, I was dating a guy in high school, and when I faced real temptation, I realized the difference in my feelings from what I had been through. I finally told my parents, and I probably didn't communicate it in the best way. Naturally, they asked me why I had kept it a secret. I'm sure this was painful to hear as a parent, and they couldn't understand most of what I was explaining. I went to them because I knew I could trust them to love me and help me. I had been trying to do it alone for years because I blamed myself for it happening. I will not lie; it was difficult, and the conversation did not go as I wanted it to. However, my mom and dad were doing their best with the information they had and how I was communicating it at the time. I never doubted their love or blamed them because I had a deep reserve of love and care they had poured into me. I knew that even when they didn't understand everything or respond all the ways I wanted or wished them to, they loved me and deeply cared for me. My parents wanted nothing but the best for me and were there to help and encourage me in that season. So often, we can discount the small deposits that build up over time with our kids, but they matter. Your children will return to what you have poured into them in their most challenging times and draw strength and direction from it. They will have a positive or negative balance based on what you sow into them. Now that I am a parent, my deepest desire is to take the actions my parents did and make more deposits of good so that they have a deep well to draw from when they need it most.

> ...MY DEEPEST DESIRE IS TO TAKE THE ACTIONS MY PARENTS DID AND MAKE MORE DEPOSITS OF GOOD SO THAT THEY HAVE A DEEP WELL TO DRAW FROM WHEN THEY NEED IT MOST.

WHITNEY

From kindergarten to third grade, my Mom home-schooled us. When I was in fourth grade, I began going to school. I really struggled because I loved my Mom and always wanted to be with her. I still feel this way. I used to try to fall asleep on the way to school so that, just maybe, she would turn around and take me back home with her. There was a time when it actually worked, and I was so happy when I opened my eyes to find myself back home. My Mom said I was so tired and that she just wanted to be with me anyway, so she decided to bring me back home. I was so excited and felt so loved to have her all to myself because she is my favorite person. She was then, and still is now because she fostered this type of relationship. She took advantage of a moment to make me feel loved and wanted. It is a little thing, but it has always been a big thing to me that has transcended my childhood.

As a child and now a mother, I see more than ever the power my Mom had/has. Now, I have to seize a moment, interrupt my plans, and show my children how they matter more than anything else I have planned. It may feel like a small thing to us, but you never know how a small decision to turn around and take your fourth grader home to spend the day with you will turn into a big thing for them that shapes who they want to be as a person.

IF YOU HAD IT TO DO ALL OVER AGAIN

Dear Parent:

So many people say, "If I had it to do all over again, I would do this or that differently." Other people have said, "Hindsight is always better than foresight." The

Spend time with me

conclusion usually involves doing something better if you could do it all over again.

Would you please be one of those rare few people, who make the right choice the first time, and thus, if you have something to do over again, you would do it the same way? Hindsight does not always have to be better than foresight.

Someone has said that when it comes to doing what's best for you or doing the right thing, do the right thing and you'll always be doing what's best for you.

Everything we do in life, every decision, every goal, future plan, involves foresight. *Foresight* is defined as, **"the ability to foresee and prepare for future needs."** *Hindsight*, on the other hand, is, **"wisdom about an event, after it has occurred."**

With both of these definitions in mind, it is easy to see why most people have more hindsight than they do foresight. If people would spend more time developing their foresight, they wouldn't have to spend as much time regretting in hindsight.

To *regret*, means **"to feel sorrow due to loss of a person or a thing."** In other words, it is wishing you could do all over what has already been done, because after taking another look at what has already been done, you see now that it could have been done better.

Hindsight for most people is better than foresight, because it is seemingly easier to look back, rather than ahead. While it may be easier to look back, it is always wiser to look ahead.

I need your hindsight to give you insight, so you can help me with your foresight.

Hindsight > Insight > Foresight

Hindsight is looking back, it's Wisdom with Regret.
Wishing things were different, but knowing things are set.
Things that could have been different, that have already been done.
Battles that were lost, that could have been won.

History is destined, to repeat itself,
Unless we are willing to get off the Shelf.
The Shelf of complacency, where everything's alright.
We must be willing to plan, if the future is to be bright.

Foresight is the ability to see the unseen.
To plan for the future, because you have a dream.
It's preparing by doing what is necessary today.
Knowing that tomorrow, Success will come your way.

Foresight is looking forward, it's Wisdom with Success.
It's planning, preparing and doing, never settling for second best.
Hindsight shows you what not to do, as you look with eyes of regret.
Foresight gives you the plan, and shows you how to be blessed.
When you ponder the question, "What would I do differently,
if I had it to do all over again?"
Use your insight today, to give you the foresight to WIN!
Your hindsight should give you insight, to know what you should do today,
To move into the future with foresight and to never go astray!

Your Child

Spend time with me

JOSH

The weekend of father's day 2019, my wife and I were at a conference in Miami, Florida. My mom texted our family that she and my dad were headed to the hospital in Destin, Florida where they were on vacation because he was feeling tightness in his chest. She told us that nothing was really wrong and they were just checking him out. 30 minutes later, we got a blurry picture that she took while they were wheeling my dad out of the room into emergency surgery because he was having a massive heart attack.

She had very little information, and my sisters and I had even less. We didn't know if our dad was conscious, alive, or functional. Keela and Whitney booked their flights from Dallas, and my wife Courtnei and I got in the car and immediately drove from Miami to Destin - a six hour drive.

Our drive began at 10PM, around the same time the surgery started. I'm not a person prone to anxiety, but when someone who matters to me as much as my dad does, is in a life or death emergency, it's just going to happen.

In my experience, when loved ones die, or experience near death, those closest to them tend to think of what they regret. They tend to see the relationship they had with their parents in hindsight. The issues that were once insurmountable somehow become meaningless. The chasms of disagreement and disconnection become nothing more than small misunderstandings. They start to think of all the ways they wish they had felt, all the things they wish they had said, and all of the experiences they wish they had with that person.

I didn't have that experience. I couldn't think of one thing I hadn't expressed to my dad. He knew how much I loved him, and I knew how much he loved me. I couldn't think of a moment we didn't seize.

When I was growing up, he would always tell us we were going to "squeeze the lemon." We would "squeeze the lemon" on vacation and do as much as we could to have fun and be together. We would "squeeze the lemon" and spontaneously take a weeklong vacation in the middle of the school year. One year I missed 18 weeks of school, squeezing the lemon. That's half a semester! My school was not happy, but I was, and so were my parents and sisters.

The only thought I had was that I didn't want my dad to go yet. There were still memories to make. I wanted to keep doing everything we were doing together. I wanted him to see his grandchildren grow up and watch them step into their destinies and have families of their own. I wanted to make more memories and squeeze more lemons with him. He is the one person who has always believed the best in me and wanted what is best for me. He has had no agenda throughout my life except what was best for me. I knew that there was no one else who could fill that role.

In the midst of all the negative emotions attached to this experience, this perspective was such a gift. To know that our relationship had been maximized was a special feeling. That's not because my parents had great hindsight. That's because they had great foresight. Because of my dad's foresight, we have that type of relationship. When I finally got to talk to him around 3AM and hear his voice, I was filled with gratitude that I would get more lemons to squeeze with him.

When I walked into his hospital room and saw him smile and reach out to hug me, I was overcome with emotion and fell to my knees like I was in a movie scene. I have never had that happen before. I told him I didn't want to do what I am doing without him and he said, *"This is my heaven on earth."* I said, *"Heaven on earth? This is my hell on earth!"*

One day, we're all going to die. God decides when our time is up. The decisions we make will decide the future for ourselves and our children. I have no regrets with my father because of the foresight he had to see the future for our family and our relationship. My dad is still going to die someday, unless Jesus comes back before then. It will still be painful for me, and for our family, but I'll have no regrets because of his foresight. I hope that I can do the same thing in my relationship with my own family.

KEELA

Unfortunately, people go through life with things left unsaid. They let time pass, holding back or pushing down their feelings for those they love most. All the while not realizing they are missing moments. One day, they will reflect and think of all they should have said or done. My dad has always taught me that "the opportunity of a lifetime must be seized in the lifetime of that opportunity," and this is where so many of us miss it. We think they will do or say it later, and then later never comes. Both of my parents are masters at seizing moments. They take action that builds their vision for the future by choosing to seize the opportunities that contribute to getting more of what they want. When you take action to create a moment instead of simply letting it happen, you are living a life that matters most to you. Ralph Waldo Emerson once said, **"The only person you are destined to become is the** *person you decide to be."* [7] I have watched my parents make decisions based on meaning and purpose. So many people never decide who they want to be, so how could they have a vision for the kind of life they want? My parents did not hold back love, affection, or encouragement. They intentionally spent time with us and ensured we knew they were there for us. Even in the middle of busy seasons, they were available to us. We knew

> **WHEN YOU TAKE ACTION TO CREATE A MOMENT INSTEAD OF SIMPLY LETTING IT HAPPEN, YOU ARE LIVING A LIFE THAT MATTERS MOST TO YOU.**

that we were the most important people to them, besides each other and Jesus.

You don't have to wait for a moment or wonder if someone knows how you feel about them or see them. You can live every day with intention and care. Life is short; if you have ever lost someone, you know what that feels like. I have seen my parents model this; it's inspiring because most people, like me, tend to hold back without even realizing it. I can go through my day and not say all the positive ways I know I should. I continually work on it because it matters that we say what we're thinking and feeling about people. Because my mom and dad are the visionaries for their lives, they don't let things, people, or circumstances dictate their responses. They lead their responses because they have made the choice to be vulnerable, to love, to express, and to encourage because it's who they are. They are an incredible example to strive to be like because, unlike most people, people in their lives will know that they love them. It won't be suggested or inferred; it will be known. This is how it was in my family all the time. It might have happened in different doses or various ways, but there was so

Spend time with me

much intentional effort made, which has built us, led us, and helped us want to model the same.

WHITNEY

One of the things my Mom would always tell us whether at an amusement park, waiting in line at the grocery store, on a road trip, eating dinner together, or just a simple day at home is, "We will never pass this way again." I remember asking her why she says that and what it means. She told me how I will never get these moments back no matter how big, how small, how hard, or how wonderful. I will never pass this way again so being grateful, seizing the moment, and squeezing the lemon is important.

Seeing life and moments this way is how you live a life without regret. Because she would always say it, I was aware of it. I knew what it meant and I saw her and my Dad seizing the moments by acknowledging those moments, kissing us goodbye and hello, never missing a moment to tell us how much they loved us, or how much we mean to them.

> ...I WILL NEVER GET THESE MOMENTS BACK NO MATTER HOW BIG, HOW SMALL, HOW HARD, OR HOW WONDERFUL. I WILL NEVER PASS THIS WAY AGAIN SO BEING GRATEFUL, SEIZING THE MOMENT, AND SQUEEZING THE LEMON IS IMPORTANT.

I got married young... at just 19 years old. I was so excited and as my Dad was waiting to walk me down the aisle he said, "Remember to squeeze the lemon today. This day is going to go by so fast and choosing to be present in the moment is so important."

On the best day of my life it helped me in that moment to

Dear Parent

choose to be present and not to end that day with any regret. I didn't miss a thing and I left the rush of the day soaking in every part. Before my wedding day, during it, and after it, this thought process helped me to be that kind of person– the kind of person that takes the opportunities to make memories, to tell the people I love how deeply I care for them, and to teach my children how to be people who do the same.

My parents had the foresight to seize every moment they could so they wouldn't have regrets. Now I don't have to have regrets either because of their explanation of it and their example.

Just a side note: As parents there are things we do intentionally but we don't always explain why we do them. You children need to hear "why" so they can see the power of your intentionality as much as they can. You may think, "They are young... can they really understand?" or, "They are older now... they don't care." They do care. They understand and pick up on more than you think. If you have a saying like my Mom did or a positive philosophy, be intentional to teach your kids what it means and why you live that way. Then don't just say it, set the example.

THE HOUR GLASS

Dear Parent:

Our time together is not forever. It is hard to fathom that someday I will be an adult just like you. I will have responsibilities, a family, and probably like most people, only time for what I have been taught by you to be important.

"*Like sands through the hourglass, so are the 'Days of Our Lives'* [8]". Life is truly a gift from God. Life is defined as, "the

Spend time with me

period during which a person functions or exists." Many people go through life and merely exist. I don't just want to exist with you. I want to function with you. God did not put us on this earth to simply exist. We were put here for a purpose: to function in an on-going relationship with Him. Secondly, to function in relationships with one another.

I want you to know that I understand how important it is for you to work. This takes up much of your time and I know this is necessary. But I want you to realize that I understand that we were put here for a more important reason than to work, so we can eat, and eat so we can work, and work so we can sleep and sleep, so we can work and work so we can eat.

Everyone lives exactly 1,440 minutes every 24 hours. If you live until age 75, you will have spent only 27,375 days, 3,900 weeks, and only 900 months on this earth. Because life is a gift from God, and not something we can apply for, the Bible says that each one of us has an appointment with death, and that no one has the promise of another day. So, if we have 18 short years together, what that means is 6,570 days, 936 weeks or 216 months. The time that has already passed, we can do nothing about it.

In closing, I would like to ask yourself the following four questions:

1. Who am I?
2. What is important to me?

3. Am I making important what should be important in my life? (Are my priorities straight?)

4. What am I doing today, based on what is important to me?

Please spend time with me, because we don't have much time together. *I Love You*

JOSH

My dad has always said, *"When you know what matters most, you can live a life that most matters."* In our family, we called these core values. I referenced them earlier in this book. When you decide to live a core-values-based life, time doesn't just pass. You are able to maximize the time in your life because you know what matters most to you. And you can teach your children the same thing.

Most people don't know who they are, so they can never help their children develop identities of their own. Most people don't have the right kind of priorities, so they live life like a ship tossed to and fro, trying to find "happiness." They model this for their children, and their children end up doing the same thing. Too few people realize that happiness is a byproduct of pursuing the right kind of priorities in your life.

> TOO FEW PEOPLE REALIZE THAT HAPPINESS IS A BYPRODUCT OF PURSUING THE RIGHT KIND OF PRIORITIES IN YOUR LIFE.

The fundamental quality that made my parents great parents was not the money they had, the things we did, or how they structured our lives. The things that made them great parents were the same things that made them great people; their answer to those four questions. Later in life, after writing this book, my dad wrote down what he calls his "Who am I" statements. Here they are:

Who are you Keith Craft?

I'm a son of God...I've been given the glory of God by Jesus! I have a 1% in my DNA that no one else has ever had...evidenced by a fingerprint that nobody else has and I'm to leave an imprint that nobody else can leave!!!

I'm an odds-defier...I was pronounced dead with a sheet pulled over my head!! God resurrected me from the dead!

I'm a Warrior for God...I'm going to fight the good fight of faith until I breathe my last breath!

I am a natural born leader...called by God to live a life of discovering, developing, and deploying my God-given potential so I can help others do the same!

I am a kingdom builder...I am generous beyond my means and live with a TO GIVE transcendent cause!

I am a Thought Leader...commissioned by God to help others elevate their thinking so they can elevate their life!

I am a best friend...constantly seeking to be my best so I can be a part of bringing out the best in others!

I am an encourager...put on the earth by God to speak God's Can Do strength into the life of others!

I am a Spiritual Father...raised up by God to be a "father's voice" to all who believe they need a voice of a father!

I am a husband to Sheila...my goal is to make her the happiest woman on the face of the planet!
I am Josh, Keela, and Whitney's dad...who has learned how much God loves me by loving them and being loved by them!

I am passionate...I am intimate...I am a lover...I am a fighter...I am a dreamer...I am a visionary...I am a believer...I am a rainmaker...I am more than a conqueror through Christ Jesus...I am a risk taker...
Finally, I am becoming...always in some kind of process that God is using to shape and mold me into His image!

These things and his core values have guided what he gives his time, talent, and treasure to. And he's taught me to write my own. Here's mine:

Who are you Joshua Craft?

I am God's son.
I am on the earth to show people how great God is. God gave me a fingerprint that no one else has to leave an imprint nobody else can leave.

I am Keith Craft's son.
I was put on the earth to turn every trail my dad blazes into a highway for others.

I am a problem solver.
I was created to invent and innovate. I help myself and those closest to me identify and solve any problem.

I am an encourager.
I know the way and show the way. I can always find a way forward and help other people do the same. I speak

strength to others.

I am a Biblical philosopher.
More than a thinker. I am a person who takes my thoughts and puts them into practice. I take my principles, values, and standards from Scripture and turn them into action.

I am a Kingdom builder
I am generous beyond my means and live to give to God and others.

I am a peacemaker.
I have the peace of God in my heart and work to bring peace to others.

I am faithful.
I am dependable, certain, and reliable. I am showing up tomorrow.

I am a trans-formative thinker, speaker, and writer
I do more than think. I have the ability to articulate my thoughts in such a way that helps other people think about what they think about.

I am Courtnei's husband
My goal is to make her dreams come true!

I am Charlie, Harper and Daisy's dad.
I always learn how much God loves me by loving them and being loved by them.

I am a visionary, I am a believer, I am more than a conqueror, I am always a champion, and I am always in the process of becoming who God wants me to be.

Making declarations like these made my dad a great dad and a great man. I believe my declarations can do the same for me. If you want to, use these as a template to write your own. When you know who you are and what matters most to you, you can blaze a trail for other people to follow. I know this for certain because I'm a product of people who did.

KEELA

I remember my parents always talked to us about the future, what was ahead, and what it could look like. They were great at being in the moment and bringing perspective to that moment because *"we would never pass this way again."* I remember when we were on a family vacation, and my mom kept saying it; the saying stuck. I think of that quote very often. It can be hard to conceptualize a moment or even know what it may mean later to you, but I remember my parents bringing attention to particular times and moments we had together. They would say, *"This is a moment I want to remember forever."* My dad often tells me that one day, he will not be on the earth and that I should remember certain things about him. I do not like it when he says this, even when writing this; I'm crying. I don't like talking like that because it makes me sad, but it is also healthy because you never pass by a moment without taking it in. My parents are so special to me; it's hard on me when they talk about how it won't always be like this. I never want to do life without them. My life is so full because of their love and their example.

I explained earlier how I saw my parents as superheroes when I was young, and truthfully, that has never changed. There is no one like them in the world. I don't feel this way because somehow, I am delusional or that they have mind-controlled me. I think I have experienced true love through them, and our relationship is so unique and special that it has changed me forever. Life with them has introduced me to God's love and helped me see what's possible in my own life. I have people to look to, people I desire to be like. I didn't have to go out and find someone to respect or follow. God gave them to me as my mom and dad, and I am forever grateful. I think there is greatness in everyone, even if you haven't had the best experience with your parents. God brought you through them for a reason, and if you will let Him show you what that is, I know you can walk in confidence like you never have before. God is always doing more than we can see. He knows how He made you, and He also knows what He has called you to accomplish. He uses imperfect people to bring us into this imperfect world to learn to love Him and others. Maybe your experience has not been like mine, but you can apply these principles and begin to make memories with your family.

> I DIDN'T HAVE TO GO OUT IN THE WORLD AND FIND SOMEONE TO RESPECT OR FOLLOW. GOD GAVE THEM TO ME AS MY MOM AND DAD, AND I AM FOREVER GRATEFUL.

WHITNEY

We all know time is precious and limited and yet we live like we are going to live forever. We treat our kids and spouses as if they will always be here, and not to be morbid, but they won't.

JAMES 4:14 (NLT) says, " HOW DO YOU KNOW WHAT YOUR LIFE WILL BE LIKE TOMORROW? YOUR LIFE IS LIKE THE MORNING FOG— IT'S HERE A LITTLE WHILE, THEN IT'S GONE."

From the time I was 5 years old I remember my Dad saying, "I already miss you!" I thought it was so silly and would say, "Daddy I'm right here!" but he knew I was going to grow up, get married, and one day have my own family. He knew how precious the time we had together was. He knew he wouldn't be here forever either. He knew what James 4:14 says.

As I have become older and especially now with my own children, I completely know what he means. I miss my kids already. Now as my kids' "Papa Gorilla" *(Grandpa's name)*, he tells them the same thing. As I watch my parents age I miss THEM already. Thinking about this causes some people to have fear, but don't see the fear as a bad thing in this case. Let the fear of what these different seasons will look like one day, cause you to have and express immense gratitude for what your life is now. Soak in what you can and don't wish your season away, even if it's a really hard one. There is always something to learn, a way God is going to use it for your good, and if you choose, there is always something to be grateful for.

My parents have always said... *"We don't have the promise of another day and we won't pass this way again."* Find the good... seize the moment... squeeze the lemon... and soak it in because, to quote James 4:14, *"It's here a little while, and then it's gone."*

Spend time with me

5

I need you to be a person of commitment

because I need to learn the value of tenacity.

BE COMMITTED TO GOD

Dear Parent:

Someone has said, *"If you don't stand for something, you'll fall for anything."*[9] Commitment is the CORE of every successful venture. Without commitment, nothing that is worthwhile can ever be accomplished. Commitment is the foundation upon which success is built.

I define **Commitment** as *"a position of the heart and mind, dedicated to the fulfillment of a specific cause with determined action."* Most people are not committed to anything except failure. Let me explain: When you have no definiteness of purpose on which you can position your heart and mind, you cannot be dedicated to any type of fulfillment of purpose. Therefore, there is no determination of action towards anything. So, to do nothing is to be nothing. Success comes from doing something. Failure comes from doing nothing. If you are doing nothing toward your Success, you are doing something towards your failure.

Someone has said, *"If you are not planning to succeed, you are planning to fail."* I believe there is no success, outside of God-success. If commitment is the foundation on which success is built, we must understand what we are committed to and why.

We have an eternal, everlasting commitment from God. He is dedicated to our success; our becoming the best that He has created us to be. He is committed unto us through His only begotten Son, that if we will do our part, He will do His part. His part has already been done. The only thing He waits for is for us to do our part.

> IF COMMITMENT IS THE FOUNDATION ON WHICH SUCCESS IS BUILT, WE MUST UNDERSTAND WHAT WE ARE COMMITTED TO AND WHY.

When we accept His love and forgiveness, and begin to understand what He has committed for us and to us, we not only receive His love and forgiveness, but so much more.

In His word to us, He says, "I LOVE THEM THAT LOVE ME;

AND THOSE THAT SEEK ME EARLY SHALL FIND ME. RICHES AND HONOR ARE WITH ME; YEA, DURABLE RICHES AND RIGHTEOUSNESS. MY FRUIT IS BETTER THAN GOLD, YEA, THAN FINE GOLD; AND MY REVENUE THAN CHOICE SILVER. I LEAD IN THE WAY OF RIGHTEOUSNESS, IN THE MIDST OF THE PATHS OF JUDGMENT: THAT I MAY CAUSE THOSE THAT LOVE ME TO INHERIT SUBSTANCE; AND I WILL FILL THEIR TREASURES." (PROVERBS 8:17-21 KJV)

What is the fruit we receive from doing what God wants us to do? What is this fruit He is talking about that is better than gold? Again, we go to His word for the answers: Love, Joy, Peace, Gentleness, Goodness, Meekness, Temperance, Long-suffering and Faith. (GALATIANS 5:22, 23 KJV)

As my parent, the most important thing I need you to be committed to is God. The seed from the fruit you bear in your life is going to be planted in me. True happiness comes from God. True success comes from being happy.

Can you see why it is important that you be committed to God? When you commit your life to God, you are committing yourself to a life of Hope in the midst of hopelessness. You are committing yourself to a life of Joy in the midst of a sad world. You are committing yourself to be governed by the Supernatural, the Unseen, which is eternal, rather than the Natural, the Seen, which is temporal.

Why do you need to be committed to God? There are many reasons: heaven, blessing, significant purpose and function in life, rather than meaningless existence, etc… But very specifically, your commitment to God will bring confidence in God and yourself. Confidence in God and in yourself, breeds eternal, lasting success.

Your Child

JOSH

"THEN JESUS GAVE THE FOLLOWING ILLUSTRATION: 'CAN ONE BLIND PERSON LEAD ANOTHER? WON'T THEY BOTH FALL INTO A DITCH? STUDENTS ARE NOT GREATER THAN THEIR TEACHER. BUT THE STUDENT WHO IS FULLY TRAINED WILL BECOME LIKE THE TEACHER.'" (LUKE 6:39-40 NLT)

Jesus teaches us a universal truth. You and I cannot lead people to places that we have never been. This passage echoes the Plutarch quote I mentioned earlier in the book. A person who is falling over cannot straighten someone else up. Unfortunately for many in my generation, commitment to God is not a priority for parents. Sundays have become "family day" for extracurricular activities, and parents often equate "being a good and moral person" as commitment to God. According to recent statistics, only 6% of self-proclaimed Christians even have a Biblical Worldview. Many parents I know were raised by parents who were committed to God and committed to the Kingdom, but they have forsaken this commitment in their own lives. They have done this, believing it will benefit their children. They think that spending more time with their kids on Sundays instead of demonstrating a commitment to God is a better idea. This is because they don't think that going to church is a part of being committed to God.

Let me ask you a couple questions. What is the most important relationship in your life? What is the most important relationship in your child's life? There's only one right answer. That's your relationship with God and their relationship with God. If a parent believes that, then they will prioritize their own relationship with God and their child's relationship with God – even above their relationship with each other. Why is this the most important relationship? It's not about being spiritual or religious. Unfortunately, most people only live in this context. That's important, but not the most important thing.

> ACCORDING TO RECENT STATISTICS, ONLY 6% OF SELF-PROCLAIMED CHRISTIANS EVEN HAVE A BIBLICAL WORLDVIEW.

Your children are not in fact your possession. They are gifts from God sent for you to steward. You and I don't own our kids, nor did we create them. Ultimately, it is not about our plan for our kids' lives; it's about God's plan for their lives. God created all of us. He has a purpose and a plan for each one of us. Your ability to understand and live out that plan is a direct result of your commitment to God.

What does it look like to be committed to God? Is it just about Sundays and church attendance? Not at all, but our lack of commitment on Sundays is symptomatic of the larger issue. That issue is a lack of commitment to building and advancing God's Kingdom. What we do on Sunday is just one part of a larger problem. Sunday church attendance is the lowest bar someone should be able to hit as a Christian. Many parents my age will delusionally say that they make God a priority in other ways than Sunday services. When the odds are, if you can't do the minimum of being committed on a sabbath day, you probably won't

I need you to be a person of commitment

do things that require more work, like reading scripture, tithing, or serving in church.

Jesus didn't come to the earth to start a religion, or to make you and I more spiritual. When Jesus talked about what He came to the earth for, it was to bring the Kingdom of heaven to earth.

Think about the country you live in. If the countries we lived in were invaded by a foreign power, the laws, standards and culture of our previous country would no longer apply. It is easy for us to think that we are citizens of the Kingdom of God because we believe in Jesus. But belief is not true commitment. I can believe in Jesus and at the same time be completely biblically illiterate and have a lifestyle that is not at all reflective of scripture.

What did commitment to God look like in my parents' life? To begin, my parents put God first with their time. The first thing we would say every morning were daily declarations based on the Bible:

"THIS IS THE DAY THE LORD HAS MADE, I WILL REJOICE AND BE GLAD IN IT (PSALM 118:24).

I CAN DO ALL THINGS THROUGH CHRIST WHO STRENGTHENS ME (PHILIPPIANS 4:13). GOOD MORNING PRECIOUS! (ISAIAH 43:4)

I wrote earlier about how my parents read the Bible and devotionals to us daily. We did this as many nights as possible. So we gave God the first, and last part of our day. They didn't do this because they were pastors (they weren't then). They did it because they valued a commitment to God.

My parents didn't just bring us to church, they served at church. My dad traveled 40+ weeks a year doing ministry, and was often gone on the weekends. I have many memories of my mom taking us to church by herself on Sunday mornings and allowing us to sleep underneath pews and sit with her in services. When we would all travel with my dad, we would be with my parents in church 24/7. We'd be in church services almost every night, late dinners, and school assemblies all day.

My parents both sought to develop a habit of obeying God and what is written in scripture. My parents didn't just read the Bible to become knowledgeable, they read it to apply it to their life. My parents taught us growing up about how to resolve conflict in any relationship through the lens of MATTHEW 18. They modeled "NOT LETTING THE SUN GO DOWN ON THEIR ANGER" (PSALM 4:4) in front of us. They taught us about how each of our family core values was tied to Biblical principles.

> BUILDING GOD'S KINGDOM WEAVED ITS WAY THROUGH EVERYTHING THAT WE DID.

Second, my parents put God first with their talent. Some Christians tend to think of their life as a list of priorities; usually, the list looks something like this:

1) God
2) Family
3) Church

My parents lived differently. What they taught us was that everything was Kingdom. Building God's Kingdom weaved its way through everything that we did. Why did we make money? To build the Kingdom. Why did we serve on teams at church? To build the Kingdom. Why didn't we play any sports or have activities on Sundays, regardless of the "league schedule?" Because our focus was building the Kingdom. Why could I be friends with certain people

I need you to be a person of commitment

and not with others? Because I needed to be friends with people whose families built the Kingdom.

Too many "pastor's kids" have grown up to resent the church. Most of the time, parents will be committed to God, but try to keep their kids separate from that commitment. In my generation, we have bedtimes, school schedules, and all kinds of other issues that we may think as parents prevent our children from being with us "building the Kingdom." No matter how hard you and I try to compartmentalize our life, work will bleed over into our family life; what happens in our family will affect work, and our commitment to God will affect everything else.

Everything we did as a family, we did together. If my parents were at a church event, so were we. If my parents were working on something, they brought us with them as much as they possibly could. This lifestyle was counter to sports leagues, school schedules, social calendars, birthday parties, and more "American" cultural elements that many families feel entitled to. So it makes sense why most parents — Christians included — will go with the flow of culture when it comes to their commitments, all because they want their kids to have friends, play sports, learn instruments and have educational and social advantages. However, the focus of the Kingdom is not playing sports on weekends, taking AP classes, or getting into Harvard. The question is not what we want to do with our lives, or what our kids want to do with their lives. The question is what does God want us to do with our lives.

> **THE ONLY PLACE WHERE YOUR CHILD'S GREATNESS CAN TRULY BE DISCOVERED AND FIND ITS FULL EXPRESSION IS IN THE CONTEXT OF THE LOCAL CHURCH.**

The primary expression of you, and your children's personal greatness will only happen in the context of the local church. The only organization that Jesus established is the church. It is the Kingdom of God expressed in the earth today. The only place where your child's greatness can truly be discovered and find its full expression is in the context of the local church. We may not all be called to vocational ministry, but we are all called to build God's Kingdom through the church. If you're committed to God, God will get the best contribution of your talents. My parents did that, and showed us how to do the same.

Finally, and most importantly, my parents were committed to God with their treasure (money). We live in a world where only 9% of Christians tithe.[10] As long as my dad has had a job, he has tithed and put God first financially. When we traveled out of a local church, my dad still tithed to a local church, even though he ran a ministry himself. All throughout the 20+ year history of our church, my dad has been a top three giver. Many years he has been the number one giver. It has never been a question for me personally whether or not I would put God first financially. I have tithed as long as I have had a job. I gave my first $1000 at the age of 16. I gave my first $10,000 at the age of 21 (my life savings at the time). Currently, at 36, I am in the top ten givers in our church. I am hot on my dad's heels to get into the top three, and get to number one. The reason I give like I give, and put God first, is because it has been modeled for me. It's not just belief, its commitment. A proven and tested commitment. That's the power of your commitment to God.

In fact, this philosophy has made its way through our entire church. Time, talent, treasure. In our church, this has become known as being "T-Rated." When we assess and measure leaders as a church, we do so according to the standard set by my parents in raising us.

KEELA

God was first in our family, no matter what. We would discuss what God says about everything and how the Word of God says to handle it. It is amazing as an adult to think back and know just how intentional my parents were about their relationship with God and modeling that for us. Now that I am older, I realize that being a role model on how to approach God was less about us and more about how they chose to be as a child of God. Of course, we were the beneficiaries of it, but they weren't putting on a show or just spending time with God because they were supposed to. My mom and dad genuinely wanted to be close to God, so that's how they lived. We didn't just go to church when it was a holiday or talk about God randomly. The things of God were in everything we did and in all we talked about; my parents intentionally brought God into our conversations daily. Parents profoundly impact their child's view of life and the world around them. Sometimes, people discount that they shape their kids' view of God. If you say something and do not live it, your child knows, and they feel the inconsistency. When a parent doesn't prioritize God, why would their child? Going to church, tithing, serving, and spending time with God are all things we saw our parents do consistently. PROVERBS 22:6 says, "TRAIN UP A CHILD IN THE WAY HE SHOULD GO, AND EVEN WHEN HE IS OLD, HE WILL NOT DEPART FROM IT." My friend's parents sometimes asked

> IF YOU HAVE EVER WONDERED WHAT IS GOING ON WITH YOUR KIDS OR WITHIN YOUR FAMILY, I ADVISE LOOKING AT WHAT IS BEING MODELED TO THEM.

Dear Parent

me how my parents got us to live how we did and show respect the way we did. My response was always something to the effect of just following what I saw my mom and dad do. If you have ever wondered what is going on with your kids or within your family, I advise looking at what is being modeled to them. I know there are some instances where you feel you have no control because your children are older and they can choose what they want to do. I agree that you may not have control over what they do now, but as a parent, you can make the right choices now. What you value will most likely be what your children value. However, you can say you value something, but if your life does not prove that you do value that through action, you do not value it. When we turned 18, my dad said he was releasing us as adults and that if we wanted him to speak into our lives, we needed to ask him because we were adults. Of course, we all wanted him to continue speaking into us when that time came because we valued his voice. We wanted his voice because he lived what he said.

I read an article recently by Tim Dinkins that may be helpful. He said, *"One of the most quoted verses about parenting is found in Proverbs 22:6. The reason it is so well-known is because the proverb is often misunderstood as a promise that guarantees a good outcome for children who are raised in the church."* " That is how I understood the verse for most of my life. I grew up thinking there was a special blessing guaranteed to families who were faithful to read the Bible and go to church. However, the original language of the verse is Hebrew, which contains an idiom that is difficult to translate into English. The verse says, "DEDICATE A CHILD IN THE WAY OF HIS MOUTH, AND WHEN HE IS OLD, HE WILL NOT TURN ASIDE FROM IT." Hebrew speakers liked to use human illustrations to describe actions and emotions. The phrase "way of his mouth" is used throughout the Old Testament. It usually

I need you to be a person of commitment

refers to what someone has said, but Leviticus 24:12 translates it as "the will of the Lord." This is helpful for understanding Proverbs 22:6 because the emphasis is on the child's will. The author is saying, *"Train up a child according to his own will, and when he is old, he will not depart from it."* Understanding Proverbs 22:6 in its original context reveals that it is a warning, not a promise. It is a warning to parents that if they allow their children to have their way, they will not depart from that foolishness when they are older. I find this viewpoint very interesting because Proverbs 22:6 should not be understood as a promise but as a warning. It is vital to realize that one of the greatest things you can do is help your child be disciplined in the things of God. Discipline is from the Latin word disciplina, meaning "instruction and training." It is derived from the root word discere, meaning "to learn." How can you help your child learn something you do not know personally? You are the primary faith trainer, not someone in your church, and if they don't see you follow God, why would they listen to what you say about God?

> You are the primary faith trainer, not someone in your church, and if they don't see you follow God, why would they listen to what you say about God?

WHITNEY

When you are a child, all you know is what you know. You think every family is like yours and every set of parents is like yours. On top of that, you think people believe what your family believes and values what you value. Until you find out...there is not always a "set of parents," not everyone believes in Jesus, and some kids don't like their Mom or Dad. My mind questioned how and why does

Dear Parent

this happen? Answer: They have parents who are not committed people. I don't just mean commitment in marriage. I mean committed to core values, personal and familial. I mean committed to their own health...spirit, soul, and body. I mean committed to living what they say and practicing what they preach.

I grew up in a household with parents leading the way who were committed to doing their best for God first. My Dad uses triads when he teaches, and he told my Mom when they first started dating that, *"If you'll be your best for God and I'll be my best for God, then we will meet at the top."* Which means, if we put God first and be our best for Him, then, in the end, we will be what is best for each other.

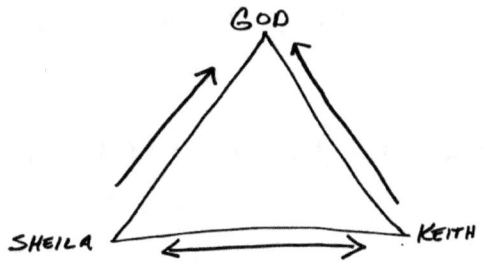

When they got married, they didn't stop being their best for God, which is why they have stayed married and committed to each other for 40 years. They consistently showed their commitment to loving each other. As kids, we always knew that their relationship came first. I think a lot of people, especially women, get this backward. They say and think their kids are first, but your kids should not be first. God is first, then your spouse, and then your kids. You will have healthier kids if you get this right. As your kids see you committing to and valuing the word of God, the house of God, and your relationship with God so that their sports games

I need you to be a person of commitment

and extra-curricular activities don't get in the way of that time, then they will know God comes first.

Also, when your kids see what I saw, which was my Dad honoring my Mom every 20th of the month with a card and flowers, prioritizing a date night every week, gushing over each other with their words and physical touch, and seeing my Mom serve my Dad his food first, it will model for them the benefits of putting God first in everything.

I realized this was them being not only great role models but truly caring for us by living their values and showing true commitment to what matters most so that we can do the same. I saw this way of living works. This principle is true: putting God first, their marriage second, and their kids third makes everything work in THE BEST way.

BE COMMITTED TO YOURSELF

Dear Parent:
I need you to have a goal and a dream for yourself. Having a goal, a target; something you are trying to reach or achieve personally, will help to give you a definiteness of purpose. In having goals for yourself, you will create for yourself the ability to keep on keeping on, when you feel like giving up and quitting. The reason most people give up and quit so quickly is simply a lack of confidence in their own ability to be committed. Either the goal isn't important enough or they don't see themselves as important enough to stay committed.

The key here is to focus on commitment and your goals can and will be achieved. The focus need not be on the significance of the goal, but on the significance of your ability to commit yourself to a specific task, and staying committed until it comes to pass. This is what being committed to yourself is all about. Because you are committed to yourself, you stay committed in other areas of your choice, and thus, you succeed and become a success in the process.

I want to encourage you to be committed to yourself. You deserve it. You deserve the fruit of labor that commitment brings. I promise you this, your commitment will be an inspiration to me. I will be confident in who you are primarily because you are confident in who you are becoming. People who are committed to themselves, develop that incredible ingredient that can't be bought or sold, called INTEGRITY. Honesty can't be bought. Incorruptibility can't be sold. The brother and sister of commitment are INTEGRITY AND CONFIDENCE.

You need confidence and you need integrity. That's why you need commitment. Without commitment, there is no confidence; there is no integrity.

Be committed to yourself.

Your Child

JOSH

Warren Buffett said *"the greatest investment you can make is in yourself.*[12]*"* I grew up in a home where my parents had a personal library full of content that was frequently in use. Most days when my dad was home, he was in his office/library studying and learning. It is still his habit today. He taught me from a young age that "readers are leaders" and started assigning me books to read as soon as I could read on my own. I have referenced previously in this book both of my parents' consistent commitment to eating healthy and exercise throughout their life.

My parents also prioritized their relationship and their own mental and emotional health as well. By doing this, they modeled proper self-care for me. I have learned by their example how to have a growth mindset, have grit to work through challenges, and understand that the lid on my life is my own thinking. My parents were focused on achieving their personal measure of greatness and that taught me to focus on achieving my own. If you desire to be great, your children will be too.

KEELA

My parents are readers, and I remember many family trips where my mom would read chapters of books to my dad out loud in the car and talk about them as we drove. This was before podcasts and audiobooks. I remember my mom and dad giving takeaways from these books and discussing how they could apply certain things personally. When I was younger, I used to wonder why they would spend their drives doing this and looking back; I realize they were growing together. My parents were always looking for ways to become the best version of themselves. Most people will never see the price you pay every day. They will never know everything you do or understand why you put effort or time into those things. Looking at my parents now, I see so many ways they practiced their greatness when no one was watching. Often, people get discouraged when they do not feel like they are automatically the best at something, and they quit. Greatness is born through hard times, and the testing and difficulty shape us. Around 13, I talked to my dad about not feeling good at something specific but was just okay at a few things. He said that he had felt the same way in his life. My dad explained to me that sometimes God gives you gifts for different seasons and reasons and that it was my job to develop those gifts and ask for wisdom on how and when God could use them. I could understand this because I had seen him do it in his own life. He was a singer, songwriter, athlete, and writer; he dabbled in acting and was a speaker. I am sure I am missing something on that list because he has done so many things, but he was always faithful in developing and deploying God's gifts when it was time. This example gave me hope because I realized I didn't need to be the greatest at something. I just needed to be the best me in the season that I was in and develop what God had entrusted within me for that time.

WHITNEY

Before my Mom was a stay-at-home Mom, she was a teacher. She has always loved kids and that has been her passion. One of the things I love and respect about my Mom is that when she became a Mom, she didn't lose herself, her drive, or her passion.

When I was nine years old we started our church and my Mom led our kids ministry. I remember serving alongside her, leading birthday songs, using a puppet, and painting stage sets. She loved every bit and she took us all along with her.

I need you to be a person of commitment

I was worried about what would happen to me when I became a Mom. Who would I become and could I still be all the things I wanted to be and do all the things I wanted to do? I had a Mom that managed that and more, so why couldn't I? Someone said to me once, "Your kids don't take away from your calling, they enhance it." This is so true and I have chosen that because my parents did.

> My Mom's commitment to her calling and to herself wasn't a hindrance to her children, but a living example of the legacy she was leaving in us.

My Mom and Dad are leaving and have left a legacy in me already... for me...in my kids...and for my future kids. We do ministry together, lead together, and serve together. My Mom's commitment to her calling and to herself wasn't a hindrance to her children, but a living example of the legacy she was leaving in us.

So...don't lose yourself, don't lose your calling, and don't stop being committed to what God put you on this earth for. In part, you are here for your children, but it's not only for them. You can show your children what being committed to yourself looks like without being selfish because they are on the journey WITH YOU! I know you can because I had a Mom that did.

BE COMMITTED TO ME

Dear Parent:

One of the greatest needs that I have is for you to be committed to me. You see, just being my parent doesn't let me know that you are committed to me.

The things you do and the things you say,
These are the things that make my day.
I will see your commitment, by the words of your mouth,
For it's in your words, that I will find faith or find doubt.

I'm looking to you, more than you'll know,
I need your commitment, if I'm to properly grow.
So many people don't stand for anything,
They are literally being held by a tiny shoe string.

In life there will be times when I feel like giving in,
I need to know you are there believing I can win.
When you are committed to God and yourself too
It helps me know that I can make it through.

I need to know you're committed to me,
That you'll help me be the best I can be.
I'll watch you be honest, I'll hear your applause,
Then I'll know you're committed in spite of my flaws.

The level of commitment you sow into me will be the level you receive from me. It will not be hard for me to be committed to you, when I know you have my best interest in mind. I need you. We need each other. I will be a person of my word, if I see you being a parent of your word. I will be honest with you, if you are honest with me. The FRUIT of God's Spirit will be seen in my life, as I observe the fruit in your life.

I really do need you to be committed to me. I may

> I WILL BE A PERSON OF MY WORD, IF I SEE YOU BEING A PARENT OF YOUR WORD.

I need you to be a person of commitment

go through some tough times. Don't despise me for this, just remind me, "Tough times don't last, tough people do."

One final note: I will never doubt your commitment to me, if I know you are committed to God and to yourself.

Your Child

JOSH

The greatest thing you'll ever do in your life is raise your kids. If this is true, then the best thing you can do is seek to love them the way they need to be loved. When your children feel deeply loved by you, they feel your commitment to them. Your children may look like you, but they are not made in your image, they are made in God's image. To be committed to your children means to help them discover, develop, and deploy who God has created them to be.

Most people want to love and be loved. The issue with commitment to your children is probably not a lack of desire on your part to love them, or a lack of need from them to be loved. The issue that we often face as children and parents is that we don't know how to love each other. I've mentioned - almost ad nauseam - how different my father and I are from each other. Our personalities couldn't be more different. He's taught me something great about love through his example: he has sought to love me the way I needed to be loved. This is the primary disconnect people experience. Not just as parents but as people. We often seek to love people around us the way that we love, not the way they need to be loved.

When we were children, we read a book called **The Treasure Tree** by John Trent and Gary Smalley to help us learn about our personality. My parents also introduced us to the five love languages taught by Gary Chapman. My parents would intentionally talk to us about their love languages as well as ours. My love languages are words of affirmation and physical touch. I have lived my life with parents who didn't just love me how they love, but have sought to love me the way I need to be loved.

Another tool we used and still use is the **Life Languages** communication profile. Through that, we learned how different all of our communication styles are. My dad has frequently said that without life languages, he would have broken my spirit growing up. If he would have communicated with me according to his language, it would have created tension between us because we don't speak the same language the same way. I think first, feel second, and act third. He also thinks first, but he acts second and then feels third. Because I "felt" second growing up, he could have communicated to me in a way that wasn't considerate of my feelings. But through the various tools that we used, like love languages, life languages, and various personality profiles, both my parents sought to love me the way I needed to be loved.

As I've gotten older, I've learned to do the same towards them, my wife, and my children. I know that my dad's love languages are quality time and physical touch. My wife Courtnei's love language is also quality time. Naturally, I

> ...IF I WANT TO LOVE THE PEOPLE AROUND ME WELL, I HAVE TO LOVE THEM THE WAY THEY NEED TO BE LOVED, NOT JUST THE WAY THAT I LOVE.

I need you to be a person of commitment

don't really care about quality time. As an introvert, it is actually difficult for me to spend time with people because I only have so much social energy. But if I want to love the people around me well, I have to love them the way they need to be loved, not just the way that I love. What says "I love you" to me, is leaving me alone. What says "I love you" to many people in my life is being with them. If I want to love people well, I have to be willing to love them the way they need to be loved.

KEELA

I always felt like my parents were on my team. That doesn't mean they always knew exactly what I needed, agreed with me in every moment, or responded perfectly to me. But I knew that they wanted me to win and wanted to help me be my best. My parents genuinely wanted the best for me in every season. I don't know if many people can say or have felt this regarding their parents, but I can. I knew that when they corrected me, they loved me and wanted the best for me. I see that this motivated correction and direction in my family. Correction did not happen because they were mad at me or frustrated; it happened because they cared enough to help me. I saw a quote the other day that said, ***"Too often, we forget that the point of discipline is to teach, not to punish. A disciple is a student, not a recipient of behavioral consequences."*** This quote was very impactful for me as a mother and reminded me of what it felt like in my family. My mom and dad didn't just discipline me because they were my parents; they loved me enough to show me they cared through the way they disciplined me. The overall message of discipline should be care; because you care, you create boundaries for your kids. Safety and freedom are found in boundaries, and too often, we cannot see this idea correctly, even in our adult lives. Boundaries help children thrive because they teach them responsibility, security, consequences, and respect, and even help with emotional regulation.

My dad talks about **Careness**, which is *"the awareness to care."* The general dynamics of a child/parent relationship can be complex because you care so much for your children that you don't want them to get hurt or make the wrong choices, so you correct them. But my dad taught us that you must show care before correcting. This may be idealistic in some situations, but the heart behind this thought is important. It can be so easy to snap at your child out of frustration or at a moment when you have just had enough.

If correction out of frustration happens too often, it becomes the central message a child receives. Through my parents' example, I have learned that leading with the positive in discipline shows the heart of careness. This awareness of care can help your children listen and apply what you are saying quickly instead of resisting it because it feels negative to them. Not every interaction with your kids can be positive, but you can always express how much you love them, believe in them, and care for them. Parents sometimes withhold this because they focus on their frustration instead of care. When your children are young, you are helping their brains be wired to understand human dynamics. They will either learn how to process emotions and care in a healthy way, or they will learn from you how to be dysfunctional. Have you ever asked your kids how their day was or what they were dealing with that day? Have you ever considered connecting with them about your personal struggles or what you are going through as their parent? Doing this helps them learn that you are a real person with real emotions. You can use moments like this as a template to teach them how to think and process their feelings.

There are many ways to connect with your child, but you can begin by stopping your everyday routine and asking them basic questions about their day, friends, and struggles. Many parents never know what their children are facing or what they go through because they never take the time to ask. This builds intimacy within a family and your child's self-confidence and identity. When you have a culture of careness, instead of taking cues from the world, they will seek you out because they know you care. I'll never forget when I came home from college, walked in the door, and my dad asked me about my day. I said it was a hard day for me, and he said, *"Really? Mine was hard, too!"* We talked about our day, and he told me he was choosing to be positive amid what felt negative and encouraged me. It wasn't a dumping session where we acted like friends or got negative together, but it was real. It made me feel like he is a real person who, like me, struggles at times. He heard me out but also encouraged me as he led himself. Moments like that growing up made me better. I don't remember what I was struggling with, but I remember the care and the connection my dad showed me. You can do the same thing for your children; it just takes some effort and time.

> MANY PARENTS NEVER KNOW WHAT THEIR CHILDREN ARE FACING OR WHAT THEY GO THROUGH BECAUSE THEY NEVER TAKE THE TIME TO ASK.

WHITNEY

I saw this video recently of this little girl at her dance recital. She was looking desperately at the crowd. As she searched and searched her eyes finally met her parents' faces and happy tears began to roll down her cheeks as her hand reached up to wave at them.

There is power in showing up. There is power in your commitment to do what you said you were going to. There is power in just being there. You have more power in your children's lives than anyone else, not only to be a model of what commitment to God and yourself looks like, but also to find out, "What makes them feel like you are committed to them?" If they are old enough you can ask them. If they aren't old enough or can't articulate it, let me tell you some things my parents did for me.

- They hugged and kissed me every morning and every night.
- When they were home they were home. They played with me, looked me in the eyes, and asked me questions that made me feel like they cared about me.
- Weekly we had family dinners filled with intentional conversation and connection.
- They made me feel like they were interested in what I was interested in by talking to me intentionally about what I liked.
- They made me feel like I could trust them and they could trust me.
- They showed up to all of my games as a cheerleader. Normally people don't come to sports games just to watch the cheerleader but my Dad did and cheered for the cheerleaders.
- They encouraged me more than they corrected me, and spoke to me respectfully just as they expected me to respect them.

I need you to be a person of commitment

- They made me feel like they were there to help me and would help me with anything I faced. If they didn't have the answers, they knew God did and taught me to pray for wisdom.

- They stayed committed to each other and to their marriage. When friends' parents got divorced or separated, they felt like those parents just didn't try hard enough or were not committed enough to each other. I know their commitment to God, themselves, and their marriage, set me up for success in life.

BE COMMITTED TO THE BEST

Dear Parent:

I need you to be committed to Being the Best; Seeing the Best; and Doing your Best.

BEING THE BEST

Being the best is something not understood.
Because if it was, everyone would.
Being the Best, is something hard to find,
It's the gold within you, and it must be mined.

There's a price to pay for Being your Best.
You can't be afraid of life's little test.
It's being misunderstood, and envied by a few.
Talking behind your back,
And with their mouths, you, they will chew.

Being the Best, involves commitment to the MAX.
It's being willing to face the sharpest ax.
Not many cheers, in your corner will be.

*But only the satisfaction known, from
Being the Best and being free.*

*Being the Best is not for the weak or faint of heart.
It's not for those who don't want a leading part.
Being the Best, is for those who strive,
For the Best life has to offer, while they are alive.*

As you can see, striving to be the best you can be, will not get you many pats on the back, or more people would try to be their best. Being the Best you can be, means not settling for the mediocre in life. It's Being the Best you, that you can possibly be with God's help. It is a Commitment to Excellence.

Can I ask you a question? How can a person be truly committed to anything, if he truly does not want to be the Best person he can be? All you have to do is take a quick look around at the problems in our world to see why commitment is so necessary. When people are uncommitted to being their Best, there is no true desire for excellence. There is only self-promotion, self-exaltation, self-destruction, and self-annihilation. It is a "gimme, gimme" world; a "me, me" focus, and the only satisfaction that is received is having more, not BEING more. This is the problem: Most people are committed to having more, not BEING more.

I don't care about having the best. I need you to be your best. Then, I will have the best.

Being the Best is a position that must be taken before you can ever, even hope, to See the Best. Most people

I need you to be a person of commitment

have a very difficult time Seeing the Best, because they have not positioned themselves to Be the Best.

SEEING THE BEST

Seeing the Best is most certainly a choice.
That will never be made by the negative voice.
Once this position in your heart has been taken.
Nothing you see can cause you to be shaken.

But the problem is not what we see with our eyes.
It's in our heart, we choose to despise.
You must guard your heart; it's a vault very deep.
What you sow, is what you will reap.

If you see the worst, and it is your right.
You'll develop a habit of walking by sight.
Walking by sight is a disastrous road.
You'll end up living, on the ground you have sowed.

Seeing the Best, means believing the Best.
It's seeing the good, in spite of the rest.
It's not judging a book by the cover you see.
It's looking inside, this is the key.

Again, the ability to See the Best, only comes after you have positioned yourself, to Be the Best. I need you to See the Best, primarily because it will cultivate for me a positive environment in which to grow, learn, and live. I also know that if you will See the Best in others, that you will look for the Best in me. Sometimes you may have to look hard to See the Best in me, but I assure you, as you do so to me, I will do unto you.

Everyone knows that there are many more negative things about us than positive. Just listen to what other people are saying about each other.

> WHEN YOU CHOOSE TO SEE THE POSITIVE, YOU ARE TAKING CONTROL OF WHAT YOU HAVE CONTROL OVER, AND THAT IS YOU.

But the real truth is this: People are only as negative as you perceive them. When you choose to see the positive, you are taking control of what you have control over, and that is you. You cannot be responsible for the negative position someone else takes. But you can and are responsible for the position you take.

This is why taking a positive position is so important, because it helps you and it helps me. One more word about negativity: It is the Cancer of the Spirit. Once you begin being negative or seeing the worst, you have condemned yourself to a life of unhappiness, discontentment, sorrow, and self-pity and anger.

You may ask, "What is Negativity, anyway?" One definition, says, "it is the attitude of skepticism." But the bottom line is, that it is the inability to See the Best, or the positive. Furthermore, Negative is a De-Motivator, a Disintegrator, a Debilitator, a Degenerator, Denigrator, a Deoxidizer, a Deprecator, a Depression-maker, a Derogator, a Desecrator, a Desiccator, a Desolator, a Desperator, a Deteriorator, a Detonator, a Devastator, a Deviator, a Devitalizer, a Delapadator; and these are just a few of the nicer names I can find to describe Negativity.

I need you to be a person of commitment

Finally, Do the Best you can possibly Do. Someone has said, that "a three stranded cord is not easily broken." When you are committed to the Best, you are committed to Being, Seeing, and Doing the Best. The Fruit of your decision will be evidenced in two areas. First, you will develop Tenacity, which is stick-to-it-ive-ness; which is persistence; which is a never give-up mentality; which becomes a never give-in reality. The only people who have true Tenacity in this world, are people who are truly committed to something or someone.

I will learn from your Tenacity, to not be a quitter, when the going gets tough. Whatever you quit, whether it is a marriage, a job, or anything, it will always give me justification, and an excuse to be a quitter. So, please don't be a quitter. I need to learn Tenacity as a result of keeping commitments I have made.

DO THE BEST
Do the Best, that you can do.
That's all anyone can ask of you.
But it's not what someone else might say,
That really matters anyway.

The person you are, when no one is around.
What you do, determines where you are bound.
The mirror doesn't lie, when you look upon yourself.
You are the one who knows, if you are a person of great wealth.

Wealth is not measured by the things that you possess.
Wealth is not measured by the way that you dress.
Wealth is not measured by the things others see.
Wealth is measured by what's inside you and me.

Doing your Best will create hope, joy and life.
The reward will be peace, instead of continual strife.
It takes more work to Do the Best.
But the reward of DOING is never settling for less.

I want to encourage you to Do the Best. Do your Best. The people who are unhappy in this world are not the people who have failed after giving their absolute Best, but people who failed, knowing that they didn't give their Best. A football team may lose a game, after they have given their best. A person may lose a job after they have given their best. But, you will never lose personally, when you have given your Best. You always win, when you give your best.

> **YOU BECOME A WINNER OR A LOSER, BASED ON THE POSITION YOU TAKE IN YOUR HEART.**

The true battleground is not the field, the ring, or the colosseum. The true battleground is the heart. For it is within your heart that you position yourself. You become a winner or a loser, based on the position you take in your heart.

When you choose to Be the Best, to See the Best, and to Do the Best, you have positioned yourself as a winner; regardless of the outcome of any situation or circumstance in which you may be involved.

I need you to be a person of commitment

When you choose to have an "I'm fine the way I am" attitude; when you choose to see the worst or continually point out the negatives in people; when you choose to live your life with an "I'll do just enough to get by" mentality, you have positioned yourself to be a loser personally, regardless, of the perceived outcome of any situation or circumstances, in which you may be involved.

Again, I want to encourage you to Be the Best; See the Best; and Do the Best that you possibly can. This will not only insure your continued success in the future, but mine also.

Your Child

JOSH

My dad defines excellence this way: *"Excellence is a commitment to be your best, to do your best...that empowers you to see the best in others, and to never allow the good to be robber of the best."*

Remember this is our family mission statement? *"Never allow the good to be the robber of the best."* Growing up, we all had different standards of performance from our parents. We weren't the family where everyone "only got A's on assignments." We were a family that gave our best. The core values that we had were a common behavioral standard that we shared. The standard of performance was different for all of us, because "your best" is subjective. When I came home from school with a B or C, my parents would ask me, "Did you do your best?" If I said, "yes," that was the end of the matter for the most part. They would take my word for it. I would have to wrestle with myself internally whether I actually did. Whitney and Keela had the same experience.

My parents could ask me if I gave my best because they gave their best. Some people live life to be THE best. When you live life to be the best, you are measuring yourself according to other people. When you live life to be YOUR best, you are measuring yourself according to the standard that God put inside of you. Focusing on being the best is actually foolish according to the Bible. In 2 Corinthians 10:12 (NIV), Paul says, "We do not dare to classify or compare ourselves with some who commend themselves. When they measure themselves by themselves and compare themselves with themselves, they are not wise."

My parents showed us how to be our best, because they focused on being their best. But my best looks different than theirs. My best also looks different than my sisters' best.

To be my best, I also could not settle for the way that I am. We had a family where our personalities weren't static. The question, *"Are you being your best?"* extended to our behavior and personality dynamics as well. There are things about my personality that I like that don't work for others. My parents demonstrated and helped me work through my eccentricities. This is important for all children. When a person is a child, there are privileges they have that aren't afforded to adults. One of these privileges is the privilege to have a dysfunctional personality. Many children today are being raised with the idea that the world will bend itself to their whims; that the world is required to gratify them; their friends and boss will celebrate them regardless of achievement; and that they are entitled to understanding and even approval for their eccentricities.

I need you to be a person of commitment

> ...MOST PEOPLE WILL TRY TO MAINTAIN THE PRIVILEGES OF CHILDHOOD, WHILE DEMANDING THE RIGHTS OF ADULTHOOD.

Unfortunately, most people will try to maintain the privileges of childhood, while demanding the rights of adulthood. My parents taught me that the rewards I experience in life will be dependent on the quality of my contribution. I will only get the best out of life if I give life my best. When you give your best you will get the best. And when you have the best, it will teach your children to give and get the best too.

KEELA

Seeing the best, doing the best, and being the best makes me think about how my parents lived this out. I could give too many stories and examples, but what stands out to me the most is that my parents lived in such a way that they created a template I could follow by watching their everyday choices. They gave us a practical example, and I witnessed them giving us their best daily. I am 35 and my parents still choose to speak positively over me and to me. They choose to see the best in me when the worst has been displayed and call out my greatness. I think back to all the ways they have been a great example, and I sometimes wonder how often they must have had to choose to lead their feelings and frustrations. Being a parent is not easy, but they have taught me that to be a followable leader, you must focus on who you choose to be every day when no one's watching. If you are not striving to be a person who lives what you say, there will not be much good fruit in your life for your children or others to learn from or aspire to. Just because you are someone's mom or dad doesn't mean that your child will continue to look up to you as they get older. My parents' example means even more because, as an adult and parent, I now see all it took for them to be this great. The strength, consistency, and mindfulness it has taken to be the parents they are is almost overwhelming. Seeing how they have chosen to live is a template for others to follow. The attitudes, actions, and behavior they have shown are examples worth following and replicating. I would feel that way about them whether they were my parents or not. What they have achieved is not impossible; it is just rare. They want to be great, so they pay a great price personally each day, which leads to them being able to help others do the same. My dad had nicknames for us as kids; they were names that spoke positively about us. So, when there was a negative moment, he wouldn't become negative and start calling names or saying negative things about us. He would use those nicknames to remind us of who we were and who he saw we could be.

My dad often told us when we missed it or how he struggled. He would relate to us in moments where most parents would simply correct. Whatever you conquer, your children should be the beneficiary of. Do not hide your wins or losses from your kids because there is a lesson for them to apply. In high school, I was not doing so well in math. I remember being very frustrated because I didn't know why it was so challenging to grasp basic concepts. I tried hard to do my best but couldn't get the grade I had hoped for. Even though my parents didn't say, *"I'm disappointed in you,"* I was nervous that this is how they would feel. I remember sitting down with my dad and talking about it. He asked me if I had given my best, and I said yes. He said, *"Then that's all that matters."* I was shocked because somewhere in

> WHATEVER YOU CONQUER, YOUR CHILDREN SHOULD BE THE BENEFICIARY OF. DO NOT HIDE YOUR WINS OR LOSSES, BECAUSE THERE IS A LESSON FOR THEM TO APPLY.

my mind, I thought he would be upset with me. I wanted to win like I saw them winning, but it doesn't make you a winner just because you get a good grade. The thought process that helped me develop a winning mindset is the core of what my dad was sharing with me. Sometimes, you won't do as well as you hoped, even when you put in effort. From that moment, I learned that things may not look like I want them to, even though I may have tried my best. What matters most is who I am becoming and what I consistently practice in my life that will be followable for others. Because of that conversation with my dad, I was empowered, and I began simply striving for my best and not putting pressure on myself to be perfect.

WHITNEY

I know reading some of this may be hard on many people. None of us are perfect and we all struggle to make the choice everyday to be our best, see the best, and do the best. For example, marriage is one of the greatest tests of commitment and being your best. We know children don't understand the intricacies of adult relationships but if our children haven't experienced commitment and instead only the rejection of it, then they will defend themselves against rejection their whole lives. They may even feel like they cannot commit because they have seen how it ends. Your children will one day have children of their own. If they have not grown up in the love and security of committed parents, then the cycle will continue, and another child will be raised without the love, feelings of safety, and belonging that having committed parents gives.

There are so many reasons relationships end. There are biblically justified reasons and sometimes it's not your choice. I get that and I am sorry if that is your story. Can I tell you that what you do now matters. The story you tell about your story matters to your kids and exemplifying commitment and being your best now makes a difference. You are not powerless and not only can you ask God and your children for mercy and grace, but you can communicate your choice to be your best now. You may not have a great track record but don't let your past dictate your future. Like my Dad says, *"Don't live life by default but by design."*

You are the architect of your family, and how they see the past of your family and the future of it, is all in the story you tell. Who you choose to be now will be in their memory too, and although you may not have exemplified commitment in the past, from this point forward in spirit, soul, and body, you can show how fast you can choose to change direction. They will remember that. My parents were not perfect but their ability to pivot quickly, to be honest about how being their best can be hard for them, and then seeing them choose to live a committed lifestyle showed me that I can too.

> YOU MAY NOT HAVE A GREAT TRACK RECORD BUT DON'T LET YOUR PAST DICTATE YOUR FUTURE.

I need you to be a person of commitment

6

I need you to be disciplined

because I need to be discipled.

BE DISCIPLINED IN YOUR LIFESTYLE

Dear Parent:
To be **Disciplined**, means *"to submit to instruction that develops self-control, character, or orderliness and efficiency."* Discipline is not a trait you are born with. It must be learned. To ever be able to learn anything the right way, one must submit himself to being taught. The desire to learn and grow is the beginning of all discipline.

I want you to understand that there is a natural desire to develop and grow within me, just as there is within you. However, there is also a natural tendency for me to do things my own way. Don't see this as stubbornness in me; rather, see this as part of my human determination to be independent. Let me stop right here and explain something to you: it is not independence that I need. You see, **Independence is *"freedom from the influence, control, or determination of another or others."***

I, like you, am not looking for the kind of freedom where I don't need anybody or anything. If I was, I would, whether I realized it or not, be headed for an isolated life, lacking intimacy and fulfillment, and eventually, total unhappiness. So, of course, I do not want to be totally independent. Unfortunately, this is the mistake many people make especially after being hurt by any person they have submitted themselves to in any way. What these people are really seeking; however, is not just to be independent, but to somehow be independent of all hurt and this is impossible.

What I really need is to bring my dependence together with my desire for independence. You see, we really need both dependence and independence. I need you and you need me. I need others and others need me. My ability to be successfully independent is in direct correlation with my ability to be successfully dependent.

What I really need then, is to be interdependent. I need to learn to be independently dependent. Please don't mistake my behavior as Stubbornness. I am determined to find out who I really am and who you really are. I am totally dependent on your ability to recognize my independence, by helping me be the best person that I can be. I will try you. I will even defy you. I am trying to find out who I am without fully understanding why I need to. Don't take this personally, How will I grow if I don't know? I need to know my boundaries. I need to know what ground needs to be developed or plowed, and what ground needs to remain fallow.

Can you see why I need you to be disciplined? By the way, please don't be one of those people who say, "DO AS I SAY AND NOT AS I DO." I will always have a hard time with this half-done, undisciplined philosophy. I can always benefit from what you say, but I will benefit more from what I see you do.

The reason for this is that I will respect you if you do the right thing and are disciplined in your life. Your disciplined life will silently sow seeds of discipline in me, because whether we like it or not, we all are influenced by those whom we are around. ACTIONS REALLY DO SPEAK LOUDER THAN WORDS. My ability to be disciplined right now, will be directly affected by the discipline you have or don't have.

Finally, please don't expect something out of me that you don't expect out of yourself. I will follow what you do more subconsciously, than consciously. When you see me, see you; then get mad at yourself, before you get mad at me. This will go a long way in helping the both of us. In other words, change you and it will help to change me.

Your Child

JOSH

I grew up in a home where my parents had few vices. They do not drink or smoke. We didn't have alcohol in our home. They invested their time and money into their personal growth and development. They invested in their physical fitness. We had gym equipment in our home. We would exercise together as a family. I remember my parents ordering Tae Bo and my sisters and I would follow the tapes with my mom. I also saw my parents work to be disciplined mentally through growth and learning agendas, emotionally in their own responses and attitudes, and with their actions. As I got older, I saw their discipline in all these things firsthand. The older I got, the more I would see their disciplined and measured actions towards people who treated them poorly or lacked the same level of emotional or mental regulation.

My parents also walked the fine line between letting me be independent and realizing that I was dependent on them. There have been stories I've told throughout this book that illustrate that point. In my view, my parents saw themselves as raising adults. Not just raising dependent children. When things were painful or difficult for me, they wouldn't step in and make it easier for me. They didn't do my homework for me. They didn't make excuses for me if I missed practices. They taught me the importance of developing grit and tenacity. They showed me through their own life the importance of delayed gratification.

In *Me, The Narcissistic American*[13], Dr. Aaron Stern says this:

"To attain emotional security, each of us must learn to develop two critical capacities: the ability to live with uncertainty, and the ability to delay gratification in favor of long range goals. Adolescence is a time of maximum resistance to further growth. It is a time

characterized by the teenager's ingenious efforts to maintain the privileges of childhood while at the same time demanding the rights of adulthood. At the same time, it is the point beyond which most human beings do not pass emotionally. The more we do for our children, the less they can do for themselves. The dependent child of today is destined to become the dependent parent of tomorrow."

The day I turned 18, my dad sat down with me and said, *"Son, I have been your dad all of your life, and I will always be your dad. But, from today forward, if I correct you or discipline you, you will have to ask for it. You don't get in life what you want, you get in life what you decide. Every decision you make from today forward will determine the quality of your life. I can help you, but from today forward, I will only help you as much as you decide to ask me."*

My parents didn't teach me how to depend on them. While I was dependent, they let me make as many decisions as I could independently, while correcting, directing, and encouraging me throughout the process. When I had my own money in high school, they would offer opinions and guide every financial decision that I made but they didn't make decisions for me; they only helped me think through the decisions I made. The kind of people I dated, the classes I took in school, my personal learning agenda and every other part of my life was an item of discussion. I was allowed to have privacy, but that didn't mean that we didn't talk about things.

> **I WAS ALLOWED TO HAVE PRIVACY, BUT THAT DIDN'T MEAN THAT WE DIDN'T TALK ABOUT THINGS.**

I need you to be disciplined

My parents also allowed me to make the decision at the end of the day. And when I made the decision, I also would experience the consequences, good and bad. My parents would always be there to walk alongside me, but they never shielded me from the results of my lifestyle choices.

KEELA

My mom and dad are consistent in what matters most, no matter what. They made the choice to be disciplined personally as well as together. Core values led what was most important for our family. I saw them make daily choices that have produced incredible results in our family and beyond. My parents would often talk to us about what they were doing and why and invite us to take action with them in various areas. Sometimes, they challenged us and pushed us to take action because we were Crafts, and they would explain we were doing whatever it was because it is what Crafts do. They held a standard of excellence in our family, spirit, soul, and body, but the most incredible thing is that they were always out in front, leading the way in each area. But I never felt like I couldn't ask them questions about their choices or why we should choose to be disciplined in some of the things. They answered my questions because they were teaching me how to be a Craft. My mom and dad did not just tell me to do things; they lived it first. Kids will naturally push back at times because they need to know boundaries. This is an essential part of developing trust and understanding their identity. Your child's life will reflect your family's lifestyle, either based on defaults or core values. Just because my parents are an amazing example doesn't exempt me from struggle. I still struggle with discipline sometimes, but I believe I am capable because of what has been spoken over me and modeled for me. My parents talked about what it means to be a Craft. They taught us the Craft attitudes and beliefs and showed us how to lead our emotions by taking ownership and receiving feedback. We often had family meetings where vision and life were spoken, but correction and direction were also given. We were asked what personal contributions we made to the family. This did not mean chores, although we had those. It was more of asking what uniqueness we brought to the family and how we strengthened it. One mistake a parent can make is trying to do everything for their children instead of calling and directing them to take action for themselves.

This is not only harmful to their future, but research has shown that children whose parents do everything for them and who protect them from taking risks actually feel helpless later in life. They are more likely to be bullied and push back on taking personal responsibility. Studies show they tend to have a fixed mindset, lower self-esteem, and a tendency to feel more fearful. Parents who empower their children through example and push them to be their best encourage their God-given identity and nurture their children's independence. Research also

> ONE OF THE SIMPLEST WAYS YOU CAN HELP YOUR CHILD BE DISCIPLINED AND INDEPENDENT IS BY ENABLING THEM TO CONTRIBUTE TO THE FAMILY.

shows that these children generally appreciate other people's efforts and respect those who do things for them instead of taking them for granted. Because of my parent's example and willingness to push us, my brother, sister, and I have not struggled in many areas most kids do growing up. One of the simplest ways you can help your child be disciplined and independent is by enabling them to contribute to the family.

I need you to be disciplined

WHITNEY

Now reading all these chapters I laugh because I see what an experiment we all were... a beautiful one. I am so grateful for parents who fought to live disciplined lives. It is a fight worth fighting. However, I believe this principle has always been the most difficult to apply.

My parents seemed to be disciplined so effortlessly. It looked like a breeze and if I am being honest, it still does. It's like they chose to be this kind of person and they brainwashed themselves into liking it! I don't like being disciplined but I have seen the fruit of it and I want the fruit.

This makes me think of farming. Everyone knows farming isn't easy. It takes hard work, consistency, and discipline. Can you imagine being on a farm with a happy farmer who loves farming versus a farmer who hates it and complains. For the happy farmer it would look effortless because he is happy to do the work it takes to gain a plentiful harvest. A happy farmer knows why he farms and plans to see good fruit. That is how my parents were/are. Happy... grateful... consistent... hard working... disciplined farmers. As their fruit, I will make sure they see a plentiful harvest until I die, by being a happy farmer also!

> **HOW DO YOU WANT YOUR KIDS TO REMEMBER AND SEE YOUR LEVEL OF DISCIPLINE?**

You are a farmer in some way. We are all trying to grow successful marriages, kids, businesses, and more. It takes hard work, consistency, and discipline but are you a happy farmer, a complaining farmer, or have you just chosen to not farm at all and see what grows? How do you want your kids to remember and see your level of discipline? Are you proud of the farmer you are? I want to be proud of the example I set for my kids. I want my kids to know what it takes but see their Mom and Dad enjoying the farming and choosing discipline gracefully, just like my Mom and Dad did. I hope one day they will do the same. My parents are experts at modeling what they were telling us to do in every area and that takes the ultimate amount of discipline.

BE DISCIPLINED IN YOUR DIET

Dear Parent:

Someone has said, "You are what you eat." In today's world, there is a growing concern about pollution, specifically the air we breathe and its impact on our climate. But we aren't the air we breathe, we are the food we eat. The quality of your diet directly affects your mental, physical and emotional health. The primary leading cause of death among adults is heart disease, which is most often linked to unhealthy dietary habits. Calories matter, but the sources of those calories matter even more.

Please educate yourself and me about nutrition. In this age of fast food and processed meals, be more mindful of the choices you make for me and yourself. Monitor my intake of sugar and opt for healthier alternatives. Outdated dietary guidelines, like the 1950 Four Food Group philosophy, are not only obsolete but can also be misleading. A balanced and diverse diet is crucial for both of our health and well-being.

We should both focus on incorporating a variety of food groups, including whole grains, fruits, vegetables, lean proteins, and healthy fats. A large part of our diet should have whole grains and complex carbohydrates, like quinoa, brown rice, and whole wheat pasta. These provide essential nutrients and energy for our bodies.

Fruits and vegetables are indispensable for maintaining good health, providing essential vitamins, minerals, and antioxidants. My plate, and yours should look like a rainbow every time that we eat. We should eat a colorful array of produce to benefit from their diverse nutritional profiles. Lean proteins, such as grilled chicken, fish, legumes, and even tofu, can help build, maintain and repair healthy muscles.

Healthy fats, like those found in avocados, nuts, seeds, and olive oil, are vital for both of our bodies to function optimally. Contrary to old beliefs, not all fats are harmful. In fact, healthy fats are necessary for brain function, hormone production, and the absorption of certain vitamins.

> BY EMBRACING A BALANCED AND NUTRITIOUS DIET, YOU WILL LIVE A LONG TIME AND SO WILL I.

As you become more disciplined in your dietary choices, you will likely find that this discipline extends to other areas of your life. A healthy diet not only benefits our physical health but also supports our mental and emotional well-being. If you are healthy, I will be healthy, if you are unhealthy, I will be unhealthy.

Please take the time to study and educate both yourself and me on what we eat. We can learn and grow together, developing healthier habits and making more informed choices about the food we consume. By embracing a balanced and nutritious diet, you will live a long time and so will I. We will also both get to enjoy our lives.

Your Child

JOSH

I can still remember my mom making us turkey sandwiches. These likely aren't the turkey sandwiches you ate growing up. These would often have alfalfa sprouts, Ezekiel bread, organic turkey, and all kinds of other stuff that didn't taste like a normal child's palate. We rarely ate lunchables, school lunches, or peanut butter and jelly sandwiches growing up. I never had bologna either. I've eaten it a lot since then, and I'm kind of sad that I missed out.

My parents were intentional in investing in good, healthy food for me and my sisters. We frequently drank smoothies and ate frozen yogurt instead of ice cream. That's not because we were wealthy, that's because our health - and their health mattered. Does that mean I enjoyed it? Not really! But today, at 36, I am grateful for it. My parents taught me nutrition without me ever realizing it. That doesn't mean I've always applied their teaching for my own life. But the older I have gotten, the more I've realized how ignorant most people are about how their diet affects their health.

I need you to be disciplined

KEELA

Growing up, my mom was very aware of and passionate about what we ate. As a family, we always ate together at night, and before we went to school, my mom would make sure we had eaten something that was fuel and not trash. My parents led the way in this area because we never had junk food in our pantry or around us. It can be normal in families to let kids eat what they want, but this was never the case in my family growing up. My parents taught us how to eat healthy and showed us why it was important. Being excellent in this area was more significant than food. We were taught that our bodies are a temple for God and reflect what we value. When I was younger, it was annoying because my friends seemed to have so much freedom. But my parents showed us how to be healthy through example and taught us that paying a small price upfront can pay off big long-term.

My mom always put so much effort into making meals for us and ensuring we ate well. There were moments of balance; we also ate out at times. But as humans, we all struggle when it comes to eating healthy. I have a major sweet tooth and would rather drink all my calories in smoothies, coffees, and other drinks throughout the day, while my siblings love food and can eat a lot at once. My siblings and I have all had our journey with eating well. This shows that you can have a great example and know the exact ways to do something to win, but you still have a personal choice to apply the knowledge you have been given. I know what to do and why I should do it, but that doesn't make it easy. I think back on my childhood and the great examples my parents were and still are today when it comes to health, and it still pushes me to want to be better. I must apply what I have learned because it matters, and it's not just to be healthy; I want to be my best for God in my spirit, soul, and body.

WHITNEY

Children have different diets than their parents in a negative way. You are eating eggs with spinach and your kids are eating pancakes. You are eating grilled chicken with vegetables and your kids are eating mac and cheese with french fries. Hungry children are the worst. BUT your kids can eat what you eat and they should. If you are eating like a toddler, then no one needs to tell you to stop... you know you need to stop.

My parents nourished themselves the best they could and we ate what they ate. Yes, it was miserable a lot of times and I remember it, but it also taught me to try things because you may discover something you never knew you liked.

A couple of years ago we were at a photo shoot for our family Christmas card and I told my kids if they would just do good, then we could get ice cream. My mom came over and told me she wished she hadn't used food as a reward but she did. She said she didn't know better and felt like it bred that mentality in us. I am not blaming her but I think she is right. Since then she has helped me with tools for my children, now that she has more knowledge. I think when you have little kids you are just trying to keep everyone alive, healthy, and happy. Ice cream helps the happy part but only in the moment.

If you read my Mom's book, *"Live Your Legacy,"*[14] you can learn all about Pom Pom Jars and how to reward your kids in a different way. It works... trust me! What we put in our mouths and in our kids' mouths is completely in our control. Choose discipline

I need you to be disciplined

happily because you know the ice cream is only momentary happiness. A healthy diet is long term with moments of ice cream happiness sprinkled in because we all need balance. :)

BE DISCIPLINED IN YOUR DISCIPLINE

Dear Parent:

I am telling you right now and don't ever forget it; I need to be disciplined. I want to be disciplined. I want to know that you care enough about me to discipline me. In other words, I want you to regulate my development. The great gift that I have in you as a parent is that maybe I will not have to go through some of the same things you have had to go through to get to where I need to be in life. I need to know that the reason you discipline me is not just because I made you mad, but that you really do want what is best for me. You will be giving me one of life's greatest gifts by letting me know early in life that there is a consequence to my decisions. I need to know the reward of making good decisions and the agony of making bad decisions.

As I have stated previously, I need you to do what you say and say what you do. I need you to always follow up on what you say, not just make threats. Mere threats will not work after a while, and that is when I will have already become a discipline problem, because you have had a discipline problem. If you are not disciplined in what you say, I will not be disciplined in what I do. What I am trying to say is that I need you to be consistent.

Let me give you an idea to try sometime that would be very effective for me in my development. The next time I get into trouble and you are saying something like, "This is going to hurt me a whole lot worse than it is going to hurt you," try getting down on your hands and knees, hand me the belt, paddle or spoon, and tell me to hit you as hard as I can three times. This will do a few things: 1) It will totally freak me out!; 2) It will let me know you are not just spanking me out of your anger, but you really want me to learn something. 3) Use this time to talk to me about how Jesus took our punishment on the cross, when he didn't have to; and 4) Explain that you don't like to have to spank me, but that you discipline me for my own good.

Of course this is only an idea. If you don't like it, that is fine. I just want you to understand again the purpose of this book and more specifically, this chapter. I want you to know at least what I think I need, or what I think might work. After all, if you want something to happen that's never happened before, you have to do something you have never done before.

Your Child

JOSH

In MATTHEW 28, Jesus uses the Greek word μαθητεύω (mathēteúō) to describe a disciple. This word means: "to become attached to one's teacher and to become his follower in doctrine and conduct of life." If you're not sure of the definition of doctrine there, it means "a belief system and body of principles".

Put simply, a disciple is a person who has been disciplined by their teacher to believe and conduct themselves in the same way as the teacher. The Bible also defines discipline in HEBREWS 12:11 (NLT): "NO DISCIPLINE IS ENJOYABLE WHILE IT IS HAPPENING—IT'S PAINFUL! BUT AFTERWARD THERE WILL BE A PEACEFUL HARVEST OF RIGHT LIVING FOR THOSE WHO ARE TRAINED IN THIS WAY."

Discipline in this verse is the Greek word παιδεία (paideía) which means "instruction by suffering and correction." HEBREWS 5 also teaches that Jesus learned obedience through suffering. Even Jesus himself had to be taught to obey God through discipline. Finally, scripture also teaches us in PROVERBS 13:24 (NLT); "THOSE WHO SPARE THE ROD OF DISCIPLINE HATE THEIR CHILDREN. THOSE WHO LOVE THEIR CHILDREN CARE ENOUGH TO DISCIPLINE THEM." Guess what discipline means here? Same thing as HEBREWS 12, instruction through suffering and correction.

Why all the scripture? Because the Bible teaches us that discipline matters. No one enjoys it. No one wants it. But everyone needs it. We need it from our parents, we need it from our coaches, we need it from our boss, and we need it from God. If we do not discipline our children, the Bible teaches us that we don't truly care about them.

We must care enough for our children to teach them the proper way to believe, and the proper way to behave. And unfortunately for us, and for our children, that requires a level of pain and suffering to learn. There are almost infinite philosophies on child-rearing and discipline.

In *12 Rules For Life* [15], Jordan Peterson says, "*It is an act of responsibility to discipline a child. It is not anger at misbehavior. It is not revenge for a misdeed. It is instead a careful combination of mercy and long-term judgment. Proper discipline requires effort—indeed, is virtually synonymous with effort. It is difficult to pay careful attention to children. It is difficult to figure out what is wrong and what is right and why.*" He goes on to state that for many parents, it is easier for them not to discipline at all because of the effort required. It will be harder in the short run for you to discipline your kids, but it will create greatness within them in the long run.

In my home growing up, we did time outs, we did grounding and we did spankings. My parents tried to make discipline as positive as possible, so we had two paddles at home. One was named "Daddy Do-Right." It looked like a 1x4 piece of wood and had a smiley face drawn on it. Then we also had "Grandaddy Do-Right," which looked like a 2x6 with a handle cut out that was taped. There is an often repeated cliché that "there is no excuse for physical punishment." If you think about it, most forms of punishment that we can name are physical. Time-outs physically remove a child from the situation. Taking a child's toys away prevents them from physically playing with them. Grounding someone in their room is physical punishment.

The forms of discipline we experience as adults are often physical. If you don't do your job, you will be fired and no longer allowed to physically work there. If you commit a felony, you will be placed in a physical location called a jail. If you misbehave in jail, you will be put in solitary confinement.

Talking to your child is not physical punishment. But what do you do when your child runs from you in a crowded parking lot? Just continue to talk to them while they are run over by a car? How will

I need you to be disciplined

> **THE GOAL OF DISCIPLINE IS TO TEACH YOUR CHILDREN TO BECOME DISCIPLINED.**

you respond to a toddler who is physically harming others and/or you? By reasoning with them? You probably won't hit them, but you will certainly physically restrain them or remove them from the situation. All of the research I have ever seen about the dangers of physical punishment is written with an assumption. The assumption is that physical punishment is done in anger.

As you read the letter written above, note that the process my dad describes is not done in frustration or anger. What matters most when you are disciplining your children is your attitude and emotional state. If you talk to them out of anger, you will say things you will regret, and/or yell. If you spank your children out of anger, you will hurt them more than just physically.

The goal of discipline is to teach your children to become disciplined. If you and I discipline in an undisciplined way, we do not teach our children to become disciplined. And they will not be disciples. How did this process play out for me growing up? First, there were 4 reasons that we were disciplined as Keith and Sheila Craft's kids:

1) Dishonoring and disrespecting my mom, dad, or other authorities - **Core Value: Honor**
2) Ongoing negativity after being made aware. - **Core Value: Positive Attitude**
3) Lying to our parents - **Core Value: Honor**
4) Disobedience - **Core Values: Honor and Excellence**

When my dad would spank me, I cannot remember a time it was done in anger or frustration. He would calmly reason with me and tell me upfront how and why I had violated the values of our family. Even though he was an intense person, he would practice equanimity in how he communicated with me beforehand.

After he spanked me, we would sit and talk about how I felt, and how he felt. There were also many times where he practiced the same technique written here. He would have me spank him and talk to me about how Jesus did the same thing. This approach was not about simply spanking as a form of punishment, but as a form of discipline. The goal was not to stop problematic behavior, it was to teach me how to think and how to act. I don't know how a child could experience this kind of discipline and not become a true disciple of their parent.

KEELA

I have always been inspired and amazed by both of my parents' choices to be disciplined. They are not perfect humans, but they are very good at being consistent with what matters most to them. This has encouraged me but also challenged me as I tried to learn from them. One of the most significant ways they taught us was by using their real-life lessons and stories to teach us not only to teach us but also to empower us to make great choices ourselves. My friends growing up had parents who thought they were leading their kids by saying things like, *"Because I said so,"* but what is interesting is that I saw these same friends make so many mistakes. All the while, their parents missed the opportunity to share life lessons with them or tell them the "why" behind something that might have helped them grow. I believe what they failed to understand when it came to discipline was teaching from their own experiences and personal life stories. This left their kids to figure things out independently and set them up to make the same decisions and mistakes their parents made.

As I said earlier, one of the most empowering things my parents did for me was teach me through their own experiences and life stories. They would tell me what they chose and why, and then they would say I had a choice on the kind of life I wanted to have. It was masterful because I could never blame my parents for my choices. This is because I was empowered to make smarter decisions than my parents at my age and those around me. You can empower your kids to be great and teach them through your life! Now that I am a parent, I am constantly amazed and annoyed at the amount of repetition I get when talking to my kids. It takes personal discipline and persistence to teach your children. People forget that **"to discipline"** means **"to teach,"** not to punish. Take the time yourself to learn how to be a great parent. You have already started by reading this book. When you become better, you help your children learn how to be great because they can look at you and be inspired by your growth. The hope is that our kids don't have to learn the same lessons or go through the same things that we have. You can help them get ahead and be successful faster than you were able to at their age because you laid a foundation for them. I was able to walk into situations and not care about what my peers said or what others did because of the weight of influence my parents had in my life. I learned from the choices my parents made and was inspired to do the same.

> PEOPLE FORGET THAT "TO DISCIPLINE" MEANS "TO TEACH," NOT TO PUNISH.

My home had no pressure of perfection growing up, and I didn't have to figure things out alone. I always had someone to talk to; I always had someone to answer my questions, and nothing was off-limits. I would often ask my mom and dad about how they handled things when they were my age and what they learned. This helped me feel confident as I made choices and enabled me to take a stand for what was right, even with my friends, because I knew someone had already paved the way for me. Because I could build on what my parents had already built, I walked with a confidence my friends didn't have. I believe God has placed you as a parent in your kids' lives as their greatest influence. My mom and dad each have strengths and weaknesses I could learn from. Being vulnerable about this, I'm sure, was not always easy, but it was life-changing for me as their child. When you let your kids see your strengths and weaknesses, it helps them to strive for even greater things for themselves. They are already learning from you each day without you even trying, but you have the opportunity to let it be intentional about it so that it brings you closer. Your greatest life lessons and wins should also be some of your child's most significant wins and lessons because you communicate them.

WHITNEY

Youngest siblings have an advantage. You get to watch your older siblings for what to do and what not to do.

I can remember three spankings in my life and my brother even offered to take one for me. My parents let him but that is a story for another time. I genuinely felt as a child that we were disciplined because we were deeply loved and believed in. It was like being trained by a coach or taught by a teacher. You know you are going to mess up but because they care, there will be a consequence, but it is for your growth. There was peace knowing all conflict and discipline in our family would always end in our relationship being better than it was before the conflict or discipline took place.

When there were spankings or any form of discipline, there was always a lot of conversation before and after. Before you got the spanking my Dad would have you say in your own words why you were getting the spanking. He would not do it until you fully understood and could say it in your own words. Then afterwards, he would cry, hug us, and tell us how much he hated disciplining us, but he had to because he knows what God has called us to be.

> I GENUINELY FELT AS A CHILD THAT WE WERE DISCIPLINED BECAUSE WE WERE DEEPLY LOVED AND BELIEVED IN.

Every discipline ended in us saying, *"Thank you for correcting me and helping me be better."* My Dad explained why we would say that, if it was hard for us to say and it usually wasn't easy, but I always would feel a shift in my heart when I would say it. I learned that saying that out loud wasn't for my parents, it was for me. It teaches your children to appreciate corrections and speaks into who they are. It says, *"We are the kind of people who are grateful for correction and direction because we always want to be better."*

As their child I would say I am grateful they disciplined me and I am grateful they were integrous in it. They never said I was going to get in trouble and then forgot or were too lazy or worn out to deliver the correction. They never forgot to have me say, *"Thank you for correcting me and helping me be better."* This also helped me to know that they would be people of their word in other ways.

BE DISCIPLINED AS A DISCIPLE

Dear Parent:
    Remember, I need you to be Disciplined,

because I need to be Discipled. ***Disciple*** is defined as, ***"One who is a disciplined learner and follower."***

I need you to be a disciplined learner and follower of the Lord. The following are the areas that I need you to be disciplined in:

1. Be disciplined in your own prayer life. Don't just pray in private, although that is very important, but also let me hear you pray. This is how I will learn to pray by hearing you pray. For instance, when you pray for me each night (and I hope you will) after you pray for me, have me pray for you. This will help me to learn not just to pray for my own needs but for the needs of others.

2. Be disciplined in your study of the Word of God. I need you to know the Word so that you can speak it over me. What you speak over me, I will eventually become. As you know the Word, it will also help you to know how to pray for me, and I will learn God's Word from hearing you speak it and pray it. This will also bring an assurance for me that you are a learner and a follower. I will be challenged to be more, if I see you being challenged by God's Word. It will be much easier for me to accept things from you, if I know you accept things from God's Word. If you pray it and speak it, I know you will be attempting to live it.

3. Be disciplined in your communication of God's

Word to me. Tell me stories out of God's Word. Read me stories. I love to hear good stories and the Bible is full of wonderful true stories to inspire and bring hope. Help me to memorize the Word. One of the best ways to do this is to pick a scripture for every letter of the alphabet. For example: **A**—ALL HAVE SINNED AND COME SHORT OF THE GLORY OF GOD. ROMANS 3:23; **B**—BELIEVE ON THE LORD JESUS CHRIST AND THOU SHALT BE SAVED. ACTS 16:31; **C**—CHILDREN OBEY YOUR PARENTS...FOR THIS IS RIGHT. EPHESIANS 6:1, etc.

4. Be disciplined in going to the house of the Lord. Please don't just be a Sunday morning Christian. I like to go to church. After all, my best Christian friends are there, of whom I only get to see, every once in a while. But don't just do it for me, do it for yourself. Sunday morning and night and maybe a midweek service are not too much to give to God for the study of His Word, is it? Most people give a whole lot more time to their job than they do their church. I don't think that's the way it ought to be, do you? Please don't forget that what you make significant will become significant to me now and later.

5. Be disciplined in your giving. I need to learn how to be blessed. I need to be taught that the first 10% belongs to God and that He is so awesome, because He lets us have the other 90% for ourselves. Please teach me to be generous. I want to be blessed.

Finally, I need to be discipled. Remember the definition for Parent, *"a source from which other things are derived."* A true DISCIPLE is one who learns and then reproduces himself in another. I want to learn from you. I will learn more from you than any other teacher I will ever submit myself to. I need your help. I need your influence, your positive influence in my life. I need you to be disciplined because I need to be discipled.

REFLECTING YOUR DISCIPLINE, YOUR DISCIPLE, YOUR CHILD.

JOSH

You will never take your child to a place you have never been. If you want your children to win, you must become a winner. If you want your children to be great, you must become great in your own right.

Your life is a template for your child to live by. How you pray will be how your children pray. How you follow God will be how your children follow God. What

> PARENTING IS HARD BECAUSE IT REQUIRES DISCIPLINE AND CONSISTENCY, AND IT WILL TEST EVERYTHING ABOUT YOU.

you teach your children about God will determine what they believe about everything in their life.

Where you spend your time will be where your children spend their time. What you do with your money will be what your children do with their money,

Someone recently asked me what is the best parenting book I have ever read. My answer was, the lives of my parents. I think parenting is hard. But it's not hard for the reasons we make it hard. Parenting is hard because it requires discipline and consistency, and it will test everything about you. Being a great parent and raising great kids requires you and I to be great people. If you are a great person, I believe you will be a great parent.

The reason many people make parenting hard is because their life is hard for the wrong reasons. They make bad decisions, they live a bad life, they are bad parents, and they raise bad children. It is my personal theory that crime rates, school shootings, gender dysphoria, behavioral issues, and all manner of emotional, mental and physical health issues can be avoided when a person has great parents.

The first question I ask when I hear about a school shooting is, "Where were the parents?" The first thing I think when I see the issues we deal with in society is, "Where are these people's parents?"

Behind every great person is a great parent. Whether that's a parent of origin or of choice. All great people have had great teachers, mentors and spiritual fathers and mothers who have shaped them into who they are today. If you don't have greatness as a template for you, you can find a great person to follow. You can set yourself as a new template for people around you. You and I need to be great. We don't need to be great for ourselves; we need to be great for all the people around us who either will depend on us, or currently depend on us. The world we live in today, is a reflection of the decisions those before us have made. The world our children live in tomorrow will be a result of the decisions we make today. Life is going to be hard anyway, so we may as well choose the right kind of hard so that the world is better tomorrow than it is today.

KEELA

This is one of the main reasons you are on earth. God has given you the kids; you have to shape and develop them. Your kids will not learn the most from what you say but from who you are and what you do. Discipline is not rules, regulations, or punishment. It is not about forcing compliance, obedience, or rigidity. Discipline is not something others do to you; it is something you do for yourself. Your child can receive instruction or guidance from many sources, but the source of discipline is not external and is inspired by what you do every day. Most people struggle with being disciplined. Therefore, they struggle to teach it to others. My parents taught me through example that discipline is not obedience to someone else's standards to avoid punishment. It is learning and applying inten-

> DISCIPLINE DOESN'T JUST HAPPEN BECAUSE YOU DECIDED TO DO THE BEST THING ONE TIME. FRUIT IS WHAT HAPPENS WHEN YOU CHOOSE A LIFE OF DISCIPLINE.

tional standards and values that help you achieve an outcome that means something to you. My mom and dad have always led the way physically, but all of us, at different times, as their kids, have all struggled in this area. This is because discipline is a personal choice, and while our parents provided a fantastic example of what a discipline-driven life looks like, we still have a choice to make. We all have weaknesses; even if you have an amazing example, you may still struggle. As Craft children, we all know the right thing to do and why it is the best thing, but true discipline means making great choices repeatedly to get the desired result.

Discipline doesn't just happen because you decided to do the best thing one time. Fruit is what happens when you choose a life of discipline.

In nature, fruit is produced when something is planted in good soil and repeatedly exposed to the sun, water, and nutrients that reach the roots. I can confidently say I am planted in good soil; I have all the knowledge to do what I need to be great. However, like all of us, I have a choice to make. I must look at what I am doing to nourish my root system. You apply the knowledge you receive by using wisdom. My parents have imparted so much knowledge into us, but we are responsible for using what we have learned. Like discipline, others won't see it; you may even feel like your right choices aren't getting you anywhere, but I can promise you-you are growing deeper. Your roots are preparing you for the fruit that is to come. As we saw with Jesus' disciples in the Bible, they had the best leader and example to follow, but they still struggled. This is because, as humans, we are weak, and we need the power of God to help us do the things we know we should do consistently. Naturally, we want what comes easy and would like a quick fix and solution. But to follow God, to be a healthy person, and to be a leader will be the hardest thing you could ever do. Being disciplined it's going to take everything you've got. Being a disciple never stops, even when times are hard. You must choose to get back up and keep making the right choice even when you don't see it working, especially when you don't feel like doing it.

This is what my parents' example has taught me. They do hard things often and keep doing them because they know it's worth it in the end. You don't need a better leader; you need to do what you already know you need to do, even when no one else sees. I have seen this set my mom and dad apart from others around me and enable people to look to them for leadership and guidance. They keep doing what they know to do, even if they do not get the results as quickly as they would like. I remember a conversation I had with my dad about this topic in my mid-twenties. I asked him for help because I was discouraged. I had been trying to learn and be my best, and I was struggling with a few challenging people in that season. My dad reminded me that I should not stop giving my best, even when others don't acknowledge it. Doing my best and being consistent is my practice unto God to be a great disciple. He reminded me that living a life that leads others will not be easy, and often, you will feel isolated and misunderstood. He encouraged me to know that I can choose to grow even in the face of opposition or frustration, and he also encouraged me to make alignments based on values. This has forever changed how I think about my role as a follower of God and even relationships. Our conversation challenged me to keep growing and doing what I know is best, no matter what others think or how they act toward me. Not everyone is for you, and that's okay.

WHITNEY

To make disciples you have to be a disciple first. Would you call yourself that? My Dad wrote, *Disciple* is defined as, *"One who is a disciplined learner and follower."* Are you a disciplined learner? Are you a good follower? How so, or how can you become that? I think these are good questions to ask ourselves. Don't just read this book and think, "Well good for them and their Mom and Dad."

We are real people, real kids, and a real family. Believe in yourself as a parent or future parent and know that you can be great! God is entrusting you with children to show them the way and to shape them. By not believing in yourself and not choosing to model true Godly discipleship, you are taking for granted the "disciples" God gave to you. No matter what, you are teaching them something and you are showing them a way of living. What do you want that to look like?

> ...AS HUMANS WE ARE WEAK AND WE NEED THE POWER OF GOD TO HELP US CONSISTENTLY DO THE THINGS WE KNOW WE SHOULD DO.

My parents decided and executed what they wanted and you can too. If their grown children can look back, and not only say they did a great job, but then want to write in their book and model their families after the way they have lived and parented... I would say that's a success and that's true discipleship. You have everything you need to be a great parent because of the Bible and now you have this book too.

I hope it helps you and I want to end by honoring my parents. They are true disciples who have lived MATTHEW 28:18-20 (NLT), "ALL AUTHORITY IN HEAVEN AND ON EARTH HAS BEEN GIVEN TO ME. GO THEREFORE AND MAKE DISCIPLES OF ALL NATIONS, BAPTIZING THEM IN THE NAME OF THE FATHER AND THE SON AND THE HOLY SPIRIT, TEACHING THEM TO OBEY ALL THAT I HAVE COMMANDED YOU." Thank you Mommy and Daddy. I love you, you are my heroes, and I hope to follow in your footsteps.

I need you to be disciplined

7

I need you to know who you are

so you can show me who I am.

Author's note
I wrote the following chapter in 2023 in preparation for the publishing of Dear Parent. More than ever, we see the effects of our children knowing who they are from a young age. As a parent, you must know who you are, so your children can know who they are. If we don't show our children, culture will.

Dear Parent:

I need you to understand the most important thing about you. You are not who you think you are; you are not who other people think you are; you are not who you think other people think you are; you are who God says you are!

I need you to know who God says you are, because it's the only way that you can show me who I am supposed to be. There are five ways that you have to know who you are and help me understand who I am. Gender, culture, personality, beliefs, and values.

Gender

When I am little, I am not sure what it means to be a man or woman. It is easy for me to be confused. I think that boys like blue and girls like pink. But it seems to me that there's a lot more to it than that. People might tell me that I'm confused about whether I'm a boy or a girl, or that I'm supposed to be something other than what I seem to be. It may sound simple, but I need you to know if you are a boy or a girl. I need you to believe that God created us as male or female and that my biology supports that. I am not assigned a gender at birth and gender is not a spectrum. I need you to teach me that the Bible tells me in GENESIS 1:27 that God created me in his image, and I was born a male or a female. I need you to see your gender as something given to you by God, so I can see mine the same way. Remember that you are made in God's image, so I can be shown that I am too.

> I NEED YOU TO SEE YOUR GENDER AS SOMETHING GIVEN TO YOU BY GOD, SO I CAN SEE MINE THE SAME WAY.

Culture

Whatever our culture, heritage, and ethnicity is, teach me to honor and value it. But also teach me that my primary identity is not my race, ethnicity, nationality, or culture. I am created in God's image. I didn't get to choose the country I was born in, or the color of my skin. God created the rainbow in the sky, He also created the rainbow of nations, cultures, and even skin colors. Teach me that all of the great parts of our culture and heritage are worthy of being celebrated. But, you should also teach me according to GALATIANS 3:28, that in Jesus we are not our skin color, gender, culture, or anything else. Show me through the way you live that our identity in Jesus transcends all cultural and ethnic boundaries.

Personality
I need you to understand your personality, so that you can help me understand mine. I might be an introvert, I might be an extrovert. I may be laid back, or type A. There are so many ways that I can be. Some of these are ways I like to be. Some of these might be ways I was born. If you're an introvert, and I'm an extrovert, do your best to let me invade your space, be a little loud and be everyone's best friend. If you're an extrovert, and I'm an introvert, allow me to be alone, be quiet, and have a few close friends. As I get older, help me learn all the different ways my personality works and value what my unique personality brings to our family, and the world.

Help me to pursue the things I'm interested in. Your job as a parent is to find ways to care about what I care about. We may share interests, we may not. Don't try to force me to be interested in what you think I should be interested in; help me to discover,

I need you to know who you are

develop, and deploy what I am interested in. You should work to love yourself and your personality. You should have high self-esteem. If you believe in yourself, I will believe in myself too. The first way I will understand how to add value is the value I add to our family. If I feel valued for who I am here, I will understand how much God values me, and I won't seek validation anywhere else.

Beliefs
What you believe is more important than anything anyone will ever tell you. What you believe about life, relationships, money, love, exercise, food, pets, God, politics, business, heaven and hell, the economy, and last but not least, yourself, will drive all your behaviors and the actions you take. What you teach me to believe will drive all the behaviors and actions that I take. The first, and most important belief is what you believe about God. How did you learn to believe what you believe about God? How will I learn? Read the Bible, teach me to read the Bible too.

> I WILL EITHER BE GRATEFUL BECAUSE YOU TAUGHT ME TO BELIEVE THE WAY GOD WANTS ME TO BELIEVE, OR I WILL HAVE TO FIGHT AGAINST A POOR BELIEF SYSTEM FOR MOST OF MY LIFE.

What you believe about God - and what I believe about God - will shape much of our destiny. Whatever you teach me to believe is what I will believe for the rest of my life. I will either be grateful because you taught me to believe the way God wants me to believe, or I will have to fight against a poor belief system for most of my life. This is why it is so important to have me in church, and around other people who believe right. Because you won't just teach me, but your friends and family of choice will too. Proverbs 22:6 says that the way you teach me to believe will be my way when I am older. If you raise me with the right foundation, I will win in life.

Values

Can I ask you a question? How do you know that you are successful? How can you teach me to be successful? I need your help to understand how to win in life. If you don't know how to win in life, I won't either. I'll think that if I make enough money, or have enough influence, I'll be successful. Just like most people. But if you raise me with core values and teach me to live by them no matter what happens, I will become successful. Teach me that I can have core values based on God's Word and I can live by them every day. Write our family values and correct, direct, and encourage me based on them. Don't just teach me what is right, but show me what is right through how you live every day. If you show me that you are a person of value, I will become a person of value.

Your Child

Throughout this book, we have written how our parents' approach to these five things influenced our upbringing and have shaped our lives. Now we are all in our 30's and are all working hard in our own ways to do what our parents did. We all have different children, different perspectives, and different approaches. And you should too.

This book is not filled with the perfect system, or steps to follow to be a good parent. Our dad has always said *"Methods are many, principles are few, methods always change, but principles never do."*

This book is a principled, philosophical approach to parenting that will help you be the best parent that only you can be. You have your own fingerprint and so do your children. God gave them to you to steward, and He gave you to them to love. Only you can parent the children God has given you.

This book is not about "how to parent" this is about "how to think" as a parent. This parenting philosophy didn't just shape us when we were raised, it is continuing to shape us as parents. We believe that our children will represent the second generation of kids raised by this philosophy. Yours can be too!

Josh, Keela, and Whitney

8

Conclusion

A Final Word to Parents

I don't think there is any person more important on the face of this planet than a parent. You aren't just shaping and guiding your children. You are shaping the future of the world. At 63, my goal in writing this book - and living this philosophy has been to help you reach your full potential as a parent. Your children need the best of you. If you are your best, your children will learn to be their best.

When I wrote this book, I was traveling 40+ weeks per year preaching the Gospel, holding motivational seminars and doing school assemblies and crusades with my team Strike Force.

Our lives have changed significantly throughout the past 32 years. We launched our church, Elevate Life, in Frisco, Texas in 2000. We will be celebrating 24 years in January 2024.

I launched my first mastermind group in 2008 and now coach over 100 entrepreneurs and business leaders. Since my 30's, I have committed my life to helping people reach their God-given potential. All of this is special to me, but I grew up watching people have this kind of success in life while failing at home.

Every success that I have in life would not matter to me if I was not successful at home. My children are the primary people that God put in my life for me to help reach their God-given potential. They all have their own lives to live, and their decisions to make.

> THE FIRST THING THAT QUALIFIES YOU TO BE A GREAT PARENT IS YOUR DESIRE TO BE YOUR BEST. AND THE SECOND IS A DESIRE TO LOVE AND NURTURE YOUR CHILDREN.

Sheila and I are confident that we did everything we could to create the right kind of environment for our kids to thrive. That is my encouragement to you as a parent. Do enough right. You don't have to do everything right. Do your best, do it God's way, and He will take care of the rest. Until your children are 18, they are your responsibility. Once they reach adulthood, they are responsible for themselves.

I cannot guarantee you that your kids will be great adults if you read this book. But I can guarantee that, if you desire to be your best, you will build the right type of environment to give your children the opportunity to make the choice to be their best.

Most children who are raised in dysfunctional

environments will spend the rest of their lifetime trying to overcome the dysfunction. The first thing that qualifies you to be a great parent is your desire to be your best. And the second is a desire to love and nurture your children.

Remember, these are God's children; you are just the steward of them for a season of their life. God has a great plan for your kids and you are a part of it. Play your part, and let God worry about the rest.

If you are a father, remember that you aren't just a presence in the home, a provider, or disciplinarian. You must be an active and responsible shaper of your child's identity, vision, and potential. If you are a mother, you set the emotional and psychological tone of your home. You are the anchor and the nurturer of your family. If you are a single parent, do what you can control and let God take care of the rest. He promises that He will.

Do your best to be a great example for your children to follow. You are your child's greatest resource and support system. For those of us who are parents, the greatest gift that God has given us besides his son Jesus is our children.

If you develop the desire and drive to be the best possible person that you can be for God, you will show them how to do the same thing. I know this for sure because I've seen it happen in my own life. And, at 63 years old, I'm watching it happen in my children's lives. What I wrote in this book is not theoretical. I've had kids since I was 28 years old. My wife and I have spent more time parenting over the past 35+ years than we have doing anything else.

Thank you for choosing to be a better parent. The world is going to be a better place because of your influence. I know you would not be reading this book, if you didn't want to be better; and for that and on behalf of your child who may never know why **YOU ARE THE BEST PARENT IN THE WHOLE WORLD!**

Thank you.
Keith A. Craft

ENDNOTES

1 Jim Rohn - "Don't wish it was easier wish you were better.... | 99stuffs. <http://www.99stuffs.com/quote/nt-wish-easier-wish-better.html>

2 Brooke Hampton – "Speak to your children as if they are the wisest, kindest, most beautiful ... – QuotesViral.net | Your Number One Source For daily Quotes. <https://quotesviral.net/love-quote-speak-to-your-children-as-if-they-are-the-wisest-kindest-most-beautiful/>

3 Ecclesiates 3:1-8 New King James Version

4 Harvard Second Generation Study (website), 2015, https://www.adultdevelopmentstudy.org.

5 Corona, Vicki. "A Quote from Tahitian Choreographies." www.goodreads.com. https://www.goodreads.com/work/quotes/39925866-tahitian-choreographies-intermediate-to-advanced-level-female-instructi Research shows Vicki Corona as most likely originator of this quote..

6 Chapin, Harry, and Sandra Chapin. 1974. Cats in the Cradle. Album: Verities & Balderdash. Label: Mercury/Mark Dodson.

7 Website: Forbes magazine, Article title: Top 100 Inspirational Quotes, Article Author: Kevin Kruse: Contributor, Author description: I write about wholehearted leadership and employee engagement, Date on website: May 28, 2013. (Accessed forbes.com on October 10, 2013)

8 "Days of Our Lives Quotes." Quotes.net. STANDS4 LLC, 2023. Web. 29 Nov. 2023. <https://www.quotes.net/mquote/715712>.

9 1945 January, Mental Hygiene, Volume 29, Number 1, "The Over-All Mental-Health Needs of the Industrial Plant, with Special Reference to War Veterans" by Gordon A. Eadie, M.D. (Affiliation: Eastern Aircraft Division, General Motors Corporation,

Linden, New Jersey), Start Page 101, Quote Page 103, Published by the National Committee for Mental Hygiene, Inc., New York. (Verified on microfilm)

10 NonProfit source. "Nonprofits Source." Nonprofits Source, 2022, nonprofitssource.com/online-giving-statistics/.

11 Dinkins, Tim. ""Train up a Child" in the Way He Should Go | Tim Dinkins." Hanford Sentinel, 4 Apr. 2022, hanfordsentinel.com/lifestyles/faith-and-values/religion/train-up-a-child-in-the-way-he-should-go-tim-dinkins/article_c4ef86a3-4292-5696-8a95-76a461f828ef.html.

12 Leonard, Michael. 2018. "How to Radically Change Your Life from the #1 Medium Writer." Medium. June 21, 2018. https://iammichaelleonard.medium.com/how-to-radically-change-your-life-from-the-1-medium-writer-e58ba14054fc.

13 Stern, Aaron. 1979. Me: The Narcissistic American. First. Ballantine Books, Inc.

14 Craft, Sheila. 2020. Live Your Legacy: Live the Legacy You Want to Leave. 1% Publishing

15 Peterson, Jordan B., Norman Doidge, and Ethan Van Sciver. 2018. 12 Rules for Life : An Antidote to Chaos. Toronto: Random House Canada.

OTHER BOOKS BY KEITH A. CRAFT

Within the pages of his motivational and inspirational self-help book, *Your Divine Fingerprint: The Force That Makes You Unstoppable*, are the tools to help you discover a unique fingerprint that you have been given. These tools will help you deploy your unique difference that your family needs, your marriage needs, your job needs, your faith needs—that the world needs. And when you embrace and live in that uniqueness, you celebrate the glory of God.

Leadershipology 101: Quotes to Live By are inspirational quotes to propel you in your leadership quest. Keith has put together his collection of leadership quotes and has included a "Keith Craft's Thought Behind the Quote" to provide an additional thought to both challenge and inspire. *Leadershipology 101: Quotes to Live By* is an excellent resource of short, life-changing quotes which have given life to people worldwide.

A hero is someone who is admired for courage, achievements, or noble qualities. This perfectly describes how Allen sees his Mamaw. Through the inspiring life and words of Allen's grandma, his very first leadership life coach, you will be shown tenets that will change your life for the better. *Mamaw's Tenets for Life* is a leadership fable that introduces you to a different way of thinking and living that will empower you to be the best YOU, you can be.

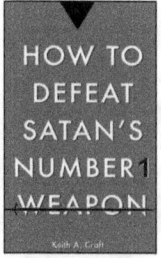

Aaron and Miriam, the brother and sister of Moses, fell prey to the ultimate scheme of Satan and unleashed a horrible spirit in the camp of the children of Israel. Yes, the devil has specific plans and you need to be totally aware of what they are. Even more, he has a weapon designed to keep you from having a right relationship with God. His objective is to strike at the very purpose of your life. With *How to Defeat Satan's Number One Weapon*, you will be equipped to win your personal battle with the Evil One.

CONNECT WITH KEITH CRAFT

KEITHCRAFT.COM

www.ingramcontent.com/pod-product-compliance
Lightning Source LLC
LaVergne TN
LVHW012045070526
838201LV00079B/1601